baen - left.
dahina - right
māila, dirty. — Thó

2/

FIRST LESSONS

IN

URDU

BY

George J. Dann,
Baptist Missionary, Bankipore.

CALCUTTA:

PRINTED AT THE BAPTIST MISSION PRESS,
1911.

PREFACE.

This little book, like my "First Lessons in Hindi," has been written to supply a need. It is intended to help those who have to study Urdu in the Persian character from the beginning, and, for this reason, in the Exercises, Vocabularies, and Grammatical Notes, that character has been used; a transliteration into Roman characters being added, as such a transliteration will be found useful to beginners. At the same time those who wish, at this stage, to learn to use only Roman-Urdu will find the book useful.

The Grammatical Notes are only introductory and elementary, as it is hoped that the student of this book will go forward to more extensive and profounder works. They will, it is to be hoped, lead up to Platts's "Hindustani Grammar," Kempson's "Syntax and Idioms of Hindustani," and other works of a more advanced character.

The Vocabulary used is that of the simplest kind of Urdu, such as will be found helpful in acquiring the language of everyday life.

Having laid a foundation of this kind, the student will find himself able to begin speaking the language, a most important factor in acquiring a sound and accurate knowledge of Urdu. Reading, writing and speaking should be cultivated simultaneously, or the student will perhaps find himself able to read intelligently, to discuss points of Grammar, and yet be unable to express his thoughts with fluency and accuracy.

A Munshi will be found invaluable for teaching to write with facility and correctness, and for correcting his pupil's pronunciation, and pointing out errors in speaking and writing, but not for teaching grammar and vocabulary. The student is, therefore, advised to master this little book at the outset, using the Munshi for help in writing, and spelling, and correcting pronunciation. It has been found a very useful plan to take a book like one of the Gospels, of which the general meaning will be familiar to the student, and, deferring translation till the *First Lessons* have been mastered, hearing the Munshi read over slowly and distinctly, verse by verse, or paragraph by paragraph, then to read it after him, while he corrects errors in pronunciation.

Then by the time this book has been digested, the student will have learnt to use his Dictionary and his Grammar, he will have got over the early difficulties of reading and pronunciation, and will find translation and speaking come easily. It is advisable to continue reading aloud to the Munshi, who should be given plainly to understand that he is expected to perfect his pupil in pronunciation and idiom. These are properly his business. If the student expects more from him, he will be disappointed. Faithful work with Dictionary and Grammar, and persistent practice in speaking, are indispensable if one wishes to learn a modern language thoroughly, and the best works of this kind are, in the end, the cheapest.

This little book will help the student to make a beginning. If he does not find all he wants in it, he may perhaps be asked to bear in mind that it is a very small and elementary work, and has therefore been made as simple as possible.

G. J. Dann.

Bankipur:
August, 1911.

CONTENTS.

First Lessons in Urdu.

The Urdu consonants are as follows:—

Name.	Power.	Unconnected Form.	Connected Forms. Initial.	Medial.	Final.	Aspirated Form.	Power.
alif	—	ا	ا	ـا	ـا		
be	*b*	ب	بـ بـ بـ	ـبـ	ـب	بھ	*bh*
pe	*p*	پ	پـ پـ پـ	ـپـ	ـپ	پھ	*ph*
te	*t*	ت	تـ تـ تـ	ـتـ	ـت	تھ	*th*
ṭe	*ṭ*	ٹ	ٹـ ٹـ ٹـ	ـٹـ	ـٹ	ٹھ	*ṭh*
s̤e	*s̤*	ث	ثـ ثـ ثـ	ـثـ	ـث		
jīm	*j*	ج	جـ	ـجـ	ـج	جھ	*jh*
che	*ch*	چ	چـ	ـچـ	ـچ	چھ	*chh*
ḥe	*ḥ*	ح	حـ	ـحـ	ـح		
ḳhe	*ḳh*	خ	خـ	ـخـ	ـخ		
dāl	*d*	د	د	ـد	ـد	دھ	*dh*
ḍāl	*ḍ*	ڈ	ڈ	ـڈ	ـڈ	ڈھ	*ḍh*
ẕāl	*ẕ*	ذ	ذ	ـذ	ـذ		
re	*r*	ر	ر	ـر	ـر		
ṛe	*ṛ*	ڑ	ڑ	ـڑ	ـڑ	ڑھ	*ṛh*
ze	*z*	ز	ز	ـز	ـز		
zhe	*zh*	ژ	ژ	ـژ	ـژ		

Name.	Power.	Unconnected Form.	Connected Forms. Initial.	Connected Forms. Medial	Connected Forms. Final.	Aspirated Form.	Power.
sín	*s*	(س سـں)	ﺳ	ﺴ	ﺲ		
shín	*sh*	(ش شـں)	ﺷ	ﺸ	ﺶ		
ṣad	*ṣ*	ص	ﺻ	ﺼ	ﺺ		
ẓad	*ẓ*	ض	ﺿ	ﻀ	ﺾ		
ṭoe	*ṭ*	ط	ﻃ	ﻄ	ﻂ		
zoe	*z̤*	ظ	ﻇ	ﻈ	ﻆ		
'ain	*'a*	ع	ﻋ	ﻌ	ﻊ		
g̣ain	*g̣*	غ	ﻏ	ﻐ	ﻎ		
fe	*f*	ف	ﻓ	ﻔ	ﻒ		
qāf	*q*	ق	ﻗ	ﻘ	ﻖ		
kāf	*k*	ک	کـ	ـکـ	ـک	کھ	*kh*
gāf	*g*	گ	گـ	ـگـ	ـگ	گھ	*gh*
lām	*l*	ل	ﻟ	ﻠ	ﻞ		
mīm	*m*	م	ﻣ	ﻤ	ﻢ		
nūn	*n*	ن	ﻧ ﻧ ﻧ	ﻨ	ﻦ		
waw	*w*	و	و	ﻮ	ﻮ		
he	*h*	ہ	ﮨ ھ	ﮩ ﻬ	ﻪ ﮧ		
ye	*y*	ي	ﻳ ﻳ ﻳ	ﻴ	ﻲ		

The Urdu vowels, short and long, and diphthongs, are as follows :—

اَ	اِ	اُ	آ	اِی	اُو	اے	اَے	او	اَو
a	*i*	*u*	*ā*	*ī*	*ū*	*e*	*ai*	*o*	*au*

Combined with consonants :—

بَ	بِ	بُ	با	بی	بُو	بے	بَے	بو	بَو
ba	*bi*	*bu*	*bā*	*bī*	*bū*	*be*	*bai*	*bo*	*bau*
جَ	جِ	جُ	جا	جی	جُو	جے	جَے	جو	جَو
ja	*ji*	*ju*	*jā*	*jī*	*jū*	*je*	*jai*	*jo*	*jau*
سَ	سِ	سُ	سا	سی	سُو	سے	سَے	سو	سَو
sa	*si*	*su*	*sā*	*sī*	*sū*	*se*	*sai*	*so*	*sau*
کَ	کِ	کُ	کا	کی	کُو	کے	کَے	کو	کَو
ka	*ki*	*ku*	*kā*	*kī*	*kū*	*ke*	*kai*	*ko*	*kau*
تھَ	تھِ	تھُ	تھا	تھی	تھُو	تھے	تھَے	تھو	تھَو
tha	*thi*	*thu*	*thā*	*thī*	*thū*	*the*	*thai*	*tho*	*thau*

The mark ْ called *jazm* or *sukūn* signifies that the consonant over which it is written is not vocalized, as *narm*, *sard*, *sust*, *gir*, گِر - سُست - سرد - نرم . *Tashdid* ّ doubles the consonant over which it is written, as *quwwat*, *ṭaṭṭī*. تَتّی قُوّت . Other orthographical signs, occasionally used, will be dealt with in notes to the exercises, as the need for explanation may arise.

LESSON I.

Reading Exercise.

Note.—Short *a* (َ) will not usually be written. Where no vowel is written it is to be understood.

اب زر رٹھہ اِس اُہ رُم

رب ڈر رکھہ رِس وُہ دُم

راکھہ ڈرا دوا آور روز اُود ڈری

ڈاک ڈُرا اُڑا ڈَوڑ زور دُور اُڑی

بک ٹل بم ھم ٹن تھن پک چل کم جھم دن جھن

چق بل سِل دِن پِس پِٹ دِق تِل کِھل گِن گِھس چِٹ

چُپ بُت اُڑ پُل تُم چُن گُپ رُت گُڑ کُل دُم سُن

لب ٹپ پٹ بج بد اُس کب گپ چٹ حجّ بھد گُھس

پر چڑ لُٹ بط دف پِھر گھر لڑ گُھٹ خط صف گِر

نام رام - ناک صاف

اور گول پھول دوب دور

دُوڑ ڈُھول بُھول خُوب کُود

LESSON II.

Exercise in Transliteration.

The following words are to be transliterated from the Roman into the Persian character :—

Din, rāt, jī, ʻaql, gīt, bāt, baṭ, chīz, roz, waqt, baras, kar, baʻd, burā, baṛā, adā, murg̠, shakk, fajr, ẕabh, qaul, ḥaqq, shām, binā, marẓ, āj, zan, sir, hil, milā, ʻalī, K͟hudā, hai, he, bil, niṣf, k͟hāss, bhun, jhīl, fíl, him, bʻaz, bish, nān.

LESSON III.

The following words are to be transliterated into the Roman character :—

صحرا - سحاب - صادق - لعاب - نصیب - شہرت -

فرصت - کثرت - وارث - ہلال - قطن - زکام - خزان - مسطر -

وصلی - تختی - مصری - جہول - جاڑا - دنیا - کوڑا - کٹورا -

گونگا - سرخاب - شاداب - یعقوب - حقیقت - طراوت - قناعت -

معراج - یاجوج - تحاشا - اسباب - عجائب - صداقت *

Transliterate into the Persian character :—

Gangā, laṛkā, mez, nangā, ṣawāb, ḥisāb, rikāb, ṭālib, gulāb, ruk͟hsat, sāʻat, raḥmat, nihāl, patthar, gustāḳh, liyāqat, ganwār, langūr, banāwaṭ, andāz, muṣíbat, jamāʻat, ḥaqīqat, galaṭī, jhūṭhā, ʻaurat, riwāj.

In the following lessons the vowel-points will not be written. In Urdu literature they are very rarely written and the student will therefore be compelled to learn to read without them. In this book, in order to help the student at this early stage, the Urdu, as romanized, is printed beside the Urdu in the Persian character. The student is advised to practise reading in the Persian character, so as to gain facility in it, as romanized books are comparatively few.

LESSON IV.

The Nominative Case.

Gender and Number.

In Urdu, nouns signifying males are usually masculine, and those which signify females feminine. To this general rule there are some exceptions, owing to the gender of certain nouns following their form, rather than their signification.

Generally speaking, nouns ending in ا (*a*), او (*a o*) و (*ū* or *o*) ه ـَ (*a*), are masculine. Terminations usually denoting the feminine are ی ـِ (*í*), ت (*t*), and ش ـِ (*ish*).

To these rules the exceptions are very numerous. For the beginner the safest rule is to learn the gender of each word when the word itself is learnt. For elaborate lists of rules and exceptions, the student is referred to the Standard Grammars of Urdu, especially that of Platts.

Plural. 1. Masculine nouns ending in a consonant are the same in the nominative singular and plural, as گهر. *ghar*, house or houses.

2. Masculines in ا, *á*, or ه ـَ *a*, change to ے, *e*, in the nominative plural, as لڑکا, *laṛkā*, boy, لڑکے, *laṛke*, boys.

3. Feminine nouns in ی ـِ *í*, take the form یاں ـِ *iyāṉ* in the plural nominative, as لڑکی *laṛkí*, girl, لڑکیاں, *laṛkiyāṉ*, girls.

4. Other feminine nouns terminate in یں, *eṉ*, in the nominative plural, as رات, *rāt*, night, راتیں, *rāteṉ*, nights.

Adjectives ending in ا, *ā*, form their feminine in ی ـِ, *í*; as کالا گھوڑا, *kālā ghoṛā*, black horse, کالی گھوڑی, *kālí ghoṛí*, black mare. Singular and plural are the same in form. All other adjectives are indeclinable.

naya = new. m.
nai = f.

Verbs agree with their nominatives in number and person, excepting in the forms noted in Lesson VII, below.

Exercise.

1.	یہ میز ہے	*yih mez hai.*
2.	وہ آدمي ہے	*wuh ādmī hai.*
3.	یہ عورتیں ہیں	*yih auraten̲ hain̲.*
4.	وہ گھوڑے ہیں	*wuh ghoṛe hain.*
5.	یہ بڑي میزیں ہیں	*yih baṛi mezen̲ hain̲.*
6.	وہ لڑکے چھوٹے تھے	*wuh laṛke chhoṭe the.*
7.	گھوڑیاں کالي تھیں	*ghoṛiyān̲ kālī thīn̲.*
8.	کپڑے سفید تھے	*kapṛe sufed the.*
9.	یہ لڑکیاں کالي ہیں	*yih laṛkiyān̲ kālī hain̲.*
10.	وہ چیزیں بڑي تھیں	*wuh chizen̲ baṛī thīn̲.*
11.	یہ بڑا گھوڑا ہے	*yih baṛā ghoṛa hai.*
12.	وہ عورت چھوٹي تھي	*wuh ʻaurat chhoṭī thí.*

Translate into Urdu :—

1. This is a man. 2. That thing is a table. 3. This horse is big. 4. Those girls were fair. 5. These boys were dark. 6. This thing is small. 7. That is (a) white table. 8. (The) black cloths. 9. Large tables. 10. (The) cloths are white. 11. This woman is small. 12. Those are black mares.

Vocabulary.

یہ, *yih,* pron. and adj. pron. com. gen. sing. and pl. he, she, it, this, these.

وہ, *wuh,* pron. and adj. pron. com. gen. sing. and pl. he she, it, that, those.

yih + wuh p. 119
us + we.

ہے, *hai*, v. sing. com. gen., is.
ہیں, *haiṉ*, v. plur. ,, ,, are.
تہا, *thā*, v. sing. m. gen., was.
تہے, *the*, v. pl. m. ,, were.
تہی, *thī*, v. sing. fem. gen., was.
تہیں, *thīṉ*, v. pl. ,, ,, were.
میز *mez*, n. fem. table.
آدمی *admī*, n. masc. man.
عورت *'aurat*, n. fem. woman.
گھوڑا *ghoṛā*, n. masc. horse.
گھوڑی *ghoṛī*, n. fem. mare.
لڑکا *laṛkā*, n. masc. boy.
لڑکی *laṛkī*, n. fem. girl.
رات *rāt*, n. fem. night.
کپڑا *kapṛā*, n. masc. cloth.
چیز *chīz*, n. fem. thing.
بڑا *baṛā*, adj., large, big, tall.
چھوٹا *chhotā*, adj., little, small, short.
کالا *kālā*, adj., black, dark.
سفید *sufed*, adj., white.

In Urdu the verb usually ends the sentence. In modern Urdu the third personal pronouns and pronominal adjectives have the same forms in the singular and plural. In the older Urdu literature, as in Hindi, the plurals are *ye* and *we*, respectively. The student is advised not to use these obsolete forms.

LESSON V.

The Verb. Principal Parts.

The Imperfect Participle and its Tenses.

1. The principal parts of the Urdu verb are :—

(1) The Root, as گر , *gir,* fall. آ , *ā,* come. کہہ , *kah,* say.

(2) The Infinitive, as گرنا , *girna,* to fall. آنا , *ānā,* to come. کہنا , *kahnā,* to say.

(3) The Imperfect (or Present) Participle, as گرتا , *girtā,* falling. آتا , *ātā,* coming. کہتا , *kahtā,* saying.

(4) The Perfect or Passive Participle, as گرا , *girā,* fallen. آیا , *āyā,* came. کہا , *kāhā,* said. From the above examples it will be seen that the Infinitive is formed by adding to the root نا , *nā* : the Imperfect Participle by adding تا , *tā* : and the Perfect or Passive Participle by adding ا , *ā,* when the root ends in a consonant, or یا , *yā,* if it ends in a vowel. The final ا , *ā,* is inflected to ی *ī,* when the Infinitive, which is really a verbal noun, or the Participle, is in the feminine.

2. The Present Imperfect tense is formed by adding to the Imperfect Participle the auxiliary verb ہے , *hai,* is.

By adding raha + the aux. hai - to root

Singular.

1. میں گرتاہوں , *maiṉ girtā hūṉ.* I am falling.
2. تو گرتا ہے , *tū girtā hai.* Thou art falling.
3. وہ گرتا ہے , *wuh girtā hai.* He is falling.

Plural.

هم گرتے هیں, *ham girte hain̲.* We are falling.
تم گرتے هو, *tum girte ho.* You are falling.
وہ گرتے هیں, *wuh girte haiṇ.* They are falling.

The feminine is the same except that the participle ends in ی, *ī*, as وہ گرتی هے, *wuh girtí hai,* she is falling. هم گرتی هیں, *ham girtí hain̲,* we are falling.

3. The Past Imperfect is formed by adding to the Imperfect Participle the auxiliary تها, *thā,* was.
By adding rahā to the aux. thā,

Singular.

1. میں گرتا تها, *main̲ giṛtā thā.* I was falling.
2. تو گرتا تها, *tū girtā thā.* Thou wast falling.
3. وہ گرتا تها, *wuh girtā thā.* He was falling.

Plural.

1. هم گرتے تهے, *ham girte the.* We were falling.
2. تم گرتے تهے, *tum girte the.* You were falling.
3. وہ گرتے تهے, *wuh girte the.* They were falling.

Feminine میں گرتی تهی, *main̲ girtí thí.* I was falling. وہ گرتی تهیں, *wuh girtī thīn̲.* They were falling.

Exercise.

1. گهر گرتا هے *ghar girtā hai.*
2. لڑکے آتے هیں *laṛke āte hain̲.*
3. میں جاتا تها *main̲ jātā thā.*
4. تم جاتی هو *tum jātī ho.*
5. عورتیں جاگتی تهیں *'auratenֶ jāgtī thīn̲.*

6.	بچے روتے ھیں	*bachche rote hain̲.*
7.	گھوڑا چلتا ہے	*ghoṛā chaltā hai.*
8.	لڑکیاں سوتي ھیں	*laṛkiyān̲ sotī hain̲.*
9.	وہ لڑکا اُٹھتا ہے	*wuh laṛkā uṭhtā hai.*
10.	یہ بیل چلتے تھے	*yih bail chalte the.*
11.	ایک عورت ھنستي ہے	*ek ‘aurat han̲stī hai.*
12.	دو آدمي بولتے تھے	*do ādmī bolte the.*

Translate into Urdu :—

1. A man is laughing. 2. Two oxen are going (moving). 3. That child is sleeping. 4. Those men were going (away). 5. I am coming. 6. Two houses were falling. 7. A horse is falling. 8. This girl is crying. 9. Those two men are waking (awake). 10. That horse is getting up. 11. Two black oxen were coming. 12. You (m.) were sleeping.

Note.—1. Words in brackets are not to be translated.

Note.—2. There is no definite article in Urdu. Various ways of expressing its meaning may be learned by careful observation of the forms of the sentences given in this and subsequent exercises.

VOCABULARY.

بولنا ,	*bolná,*	v. intransitive,	to speak.
گرنا ,	*girnā,*	,, ,,	to fall.
آنا ,	*ānā,*	,, ,,	to come.
جانا ,	*jana,*	,, ,,	to go away, depart.
چلنا	*chalnā,*	,, ,,	to go along, move.
جاگنا ,	*jāgnā,*	,, ,,	to awake, be awake.
رونا ,	*ronā,*	,, ,,	to cry, weep.
سونا ,	*sonā,*	,, ,,	to sleep.

اوٹھنا,	*uṭhnā,*	v. intransitive,	to get up, rise.
ھنسنا,	*hansnā,*	,, ,,	to laugh.
گھر,	*ghar,*	n. masc.	house.
بچا,	*bachchā,*	,, ,,	child, infant.
بیل,	*bail,*	,, ,,	ox.
ایک,	*ek,*	adj.	one.
دو,	*dò,*	,,	two.

LESSON VI.

Tenses from the Perfect or Passive Participle.

Intransitive Verbs.

1. The Past Indefinite is identical in form with the Perfect Participle, which, in the case of intransitive verbs, is inflected to agree in gender and number with its nominative, as:—

Singular.

1. میں گرا, *main girā,* I fell.
2. تو گرا, *tū girā,* Thou didst fall.
3. وہ گرا, *wuh girā,* He fell.

Plural.

1. ہم گرے, *ham gire.* We fell.
2. تم گرے, *tum gire.* You fell.
3. وہ گرے, *wuh gire.* They fell.

Feminine میں گري, *main girí,* I fell. ہم گریں, *ham girín,* we fell, etc.

2. The Present or Proximate Perfect is formed by

adding the auxiliary ھے, *hai*, to the Perfect Participle, and, ا

3. The Past or Remote Perfect by adding تھا, *thā*, to the Perfect Participle. These constructions also are used with intransitive verbs only.

PRESENT PERFECT.

Singular.

1. میں گرا ھوں, *maiṉ girā hūṉ*. I have fallen.
2. تو گرا ھے, *tū girā hai*. Thou hast fallen.
3. وہ گرا ھے, *wuh girā hai*. He has fallen.

Plural.

1. ھم گرے ھیں, *ham gire haiṉ*. We have fallen.
2. تم گرے ھو, *tum gire ho*. You have fallen.
3. وہ گرے ھیں, *wuh gire haiṉ*. They have fallen.

Feminine 3 singular وہ گري ھے, *wuh girí hai*, she has fallen, etc.

PAST PERFECT.

Singular.

1. میں گرا تھا, *maiṉ girā thā*. I had fallen.
2. تو گرا تھا, *tū girā thā*. Thou hadst fallen.
3. وہ گرا تھا, *wuh girā thā*. He had fallen.

Plural.

1. ھم گرے تھے, *ham gire the*. We had fallen.
2. تم گرے تھے, *tum gire the*. You had fallen.
3. وہ گرے تھے, *wuh gire the*. They had fallen.

Feminine singular 3 وہ گري تھی, *wuh girí thí*, she had fallen, etc.

The Indefinite Perfect is comparatively little used. The Present and Past Perfect, or as they are called by Indian grammarians, the Past Proximate and Past Remote, divide most of the work between them, according as the action, etc., of the verb is regarded as having taken place a shorter or longer time ago.

Note.—After a vowel, the terminations ـے and ـی (*ye* and *yí*) are not fully written and pronounced, but the orthographical sign ء *hamza* is used instead, as لیئے, *lie*, instead of لییے, *liye*.

EXERCISE.

1.	عورت بولي	*'aurat bolī.*
2.	مرد اُٹھا تھا	*mard uṭhā thā.*
3.	یہ پھل گرے ھیں	*yih phal gire hain̲.*
4.	وہ کپڑے یہاں پڑے تھے	*wuh kapṛe yahān̲ paṛe the.*
5.	نوکر کہاں گئے ھیں	*naukar kahān̲ gaye hain̲.*
6.	مالک وھاں سویا تھا	*mālik wahān̲ soyā thā.*
7.	دو لال کتابیں یہاں گریں	*do lāl kitāben̲ yahān girín̲.*
8.	پھول کھلے ھیں	*phūl khile hain̲.*
9.	سب بانس پھٹے تھے	*sab bān̲s phaṭe the.*
10.	بہت بچّے روئے	*bahut bachche roye (róe).*
11.	میز ٹوٹي ھے	*mez ṭūṭī hai.*
12.	جانور بولتے تھے	*jānwār bole the.*

Translate into Urdu:—

1. (The) men had spoken. 2. All (the) women wept. 3. Many clothes had split. 4. (The) master fell. 5. (The) servants got up. 6. All (the) children have slept. 7. (The) oxen had fallen. 8. A book is lying (translate

with present perfect of پڑنا *paṛnā*) here. 9. Two red fruits have fallen. 10. All (the) yellow flowers have bloomed. 11. All (the) servants have awaked. 12. (The) bamboo has been broken.

Vocabulary.

کھلنا,	*khilnā,*	v. int.	to open (flowers), bloom.
بولنا	*bolnā,*	,, ,,	to speak (to utter a sound). This word applies to animals and inanimate things as well as to human beings, as, the cock crows, the chair creaks, the man speaks ; all are expressed by *bolnā.*
پڑنا,	*paṛnā,*	v. int.	to lie, to be lying.
گیا,	*gayā,*	,, ,,	(perfect participle of *jānā*) gone.
ٹوٹنا,	*ṭūṭnā,*	,, ,,	to break, be broken.
پھٹنا,	*phaṭnā,*	,, ,,	to split, to be torn.
مرد,	*mard,*	n. mas.	man, as distinguished from woman.
پھل,	*phal,*	,, ,,	fruit.
نوکر,	*naukar,*	,, ,,	servant.
مالک,	*mālik,*	,, ,,	master.
کتاب	*kitāb,*	,, fem.	book.
پھول,	*phúl,*	,, m.	flower.
بانس,	*bāṇs,*	,, ,,	bamboo.
جانور,	*jānwar,*	,, ,,	animal.
یہاں,	*yahā<u>n</u>,*	adv.	here.
وھاں,	*wahā<u>n</u>,*	,,	there.
کہاں,	*kahā<u>n</u>,*	,,	where ?
سب,	*sab,*	adj.	all.
بہت,	*bahut,*	,,	many.
پیلا,	*pīlā,*	,,	yellow (Hindí).
زرد,	*zard,*	,,	,, (Persian).
لال,	*lāl,*	,,	red (H.).
سرخ,	*sur<u>kh</u>,*	,,	,, (P.).

The words in these vocabularies marked "Hindi" or "h" are usually those understood by all classes. The Persian alternatives are usually employed in Urdu literature and are preferred by educated Mohammadans.

LESSON VII.

Transitive Verbs. Tenses formed with the Perfect Participle.

Agent and Accusative Cases.

1. There is no Active Perfect Participle in Urdu. The Perfect Participle, like its original in Sanskrit, is really a Passive Participle, and has that title in Urdu Grammar (*ism maf'ul*, اسم مفعول). In order to form the Perfect tenses of the Transitive Verb a construction like that of the English Passive is used. The Participle is made to agree in gender and number with the object or patient and not with the subject or agent of the verb, and the doer of the action is signified by affixing the particle نے, *ne*, the sign of the agent case, as it is called by European Grammarians. The Perfect Participle and its auxiliaries agree with the object in gender and number, unless the object is constructed with the particle کو, *ko*, in which case the verbal forms are in the masculine singular.

The following sentences will illustrate this construction:—

مرد نے کھانا کھایا ہے ,	*mard ne khānā khāyā hai.*	The man has eaten food.
مرد نے روٹی کھائی ہے ,	*mard ne roṭí khá,í hai.*	The man has eaten bread.
عورت نے پھول دیکھا تھا ,	*'aurat ne phūl dekhā thā.*	The woman has seen (a) flower.
عورت نے پھول دیکھے تھے ,	*'aurat ne phūl dekhe the.*	The woman had seen flowers.
آدمیوں نے ٹوپیاں دیکھی ہیں ,	*ādmīoṉ ne topiyán dekhī haiṉ.*	The men have seen (the) hats.

With کو , *ko.*

لڑکے نے لڑکی کو مارا ہے ,	*laṛke ne laṛkí ko mārā hai.*	The boy has struck the girl.
لڑکی نے لڑکے کو مارا ہے ,	*laṛkí ne laṛke ko mārā hai.*	The girl has struck the boy.
ماں نے لڑکوں کو دیکھا تھا ,	*māṉ ne laṛkon ko dekhā thā.*	The mother had seen the boys.
باپ نے لڑکیوں کو دیکھا تھا ,	*bāp ne larkiyoṉ ko dekhā thā.*	The father had seen the girls.

2. The object of the verb or accusative is either identical in form with the nominative, or the particle کو, *ko*, is affixed. The use, or otherwise, of this particle is one of the most delicate points of Urdu idiom. For the present the learner is advised to confine the use of کو, *ko*, to persons, as in the specimen sentences above given. In subsequent lessons further hints will be given.

3. Before affixing any of the particles (like نے, *ne*, and کو, *ko*), which signify case relations, the noun is inflected, when capable of inflection. The inflected form is called the *oblique* or *formative*.

	Nom. Sing.	*Formative Sing.*
Masc. inflected.	لڑکا, *laṛkā.*	لڑکے (کو), *laṛke (ko).*
Fem. inflected.	بات, *bāt.*	بات (کو), *bāt (ko).*
Masc. uninflected.	بیل, *bail.*	بیل (کو), *bail (ko).*

	Nom. Plural.	*Formative Plural.*
Masc. inflected.	لڑکے, *laṛke.*	لڑکوں (کو), *laṛkoṉ (ko).*
Fem. inflected.	باتیں, *bāteṉ.*	باتوں (کو), *bātoṉ (ko).*
Masc. uninflected.	بیل, *bail.*	بیلوں (کو), *bailoṉ (ko).*

4. The pronouns are inflected as follows:—

Agent sing.
- 1st pers. میں نے, *maiṉ ne.*
- 2nd ,, تونے, *tūne.*
- 3rd ,, اِسنے, *is ne,* اُسنے, *us ne.*

Agent plural
- 1st pers. ھمنے, *ham ne.*
- 2nd ,, تمنے, *tum ne.*
- 3rd ,, اِنہوں نے, *inhoṉ ne,* اُونہوں نے, *un hoṉ ne.*

Acc. sing.
- 1st pers. مجھکو, *mujh ko.* / مجھے, *mujhe.*
- 2nd ,, تجھکو, *tujh ko.* / تجھے, *tujhe.*

Acc. sing. 3rd pers. { اِسکو , *is ko*, اُسکو , *us ko.*
{ اِسے , *ise*, اُسے , *use.*

Acc. plural
- 1st ,, { ھمکو , *ham ko.* / ھمیں , *hamen̲.*
- 2nd ,, { تمکو , *tum ko.* / تمہیں .
- 3rd ,, { اِنکو , *in ko*, اِنہیں , *inhen̲.* / اُنکو , *un ko*, اُنہیں , *unhen̲.*

5. When the pronouns are used adjectively the order is :—

(1) Adjective pronoun. (2) The Noun qualified. (3) The affixed particle, as اس آدمي نے مارا ھے , *is ádmí ne mārā hai.* This man has struck.

6. The student will be relieved to know that there are only the six following verbs in Urdu which are irregular. The irregularity is in the Perfect Participle and the tenses formed from it.

ھونا , *honá*,	pf. pt.	ھوا , *huá*,	to become.
مرنا , *marná*,	,, ,,	موا , *muá*,	to die. Márna - to beat
جانا , *jáná*,	,, ,,	گیا , *gayá*,	to go.
کرنا , *karná*,	,, ,,	کیا , *kiyá*,	to do.
دینا , *dená*,	,, ,,	دیا , *diyá*;	to give.
لینا , *lená*,	,, ,,	لیا , *liyá*,	to take.

EXERCISE.

1. میں نے گھر بنائے ھیں *main ne ghar banāye hain̲.*
2. آدمي نے مجھکو مارا تھا *ādmī ne mujh ko mārā thā.*
3. عورتوں نے دو کتابیں پڑھي تھیں *ʻauraton̲ ne do kitaben̲ paṛhi thīn̲.*

4.	بیلوں نے گھاس کھای ھے	*bailon̲ ne ghās khāī hai.*
5.	لڑکی نے کھانا پکایا ھے	*laṛkī ne khānā pakāyā hai.*
6.	سانپ نے لڑکي کو کاٹا تھا	*sāṉp ne laṛkí ko kāṭā thā.*
7.	اُنھوں نے دو بڑے گھر بنائے ھیں	*unhon̲ ne do baṛe ghar banāye haīn̲.*
8.	اُس آدمي نے تین لڑکوں کو بلایا ھے	*us ādmī ne tín laṛkon̲ ko bulāyā hai.*
9.	تم نے یہ باتیں نہیں کہیں	*tum ne yih bāten̲ nahīn̲ kahīn̲.*
10.	اُنھوں نے کیا کیا تھا	*unhon̲ ne kyā kiyā thā.*
11.	اُس نے روٹي دي ھے	*us ne roṭi dī hai.*
12.	ھم نے اُن آدمیوں کو دیکھا تھا	*ham ne un admion̲ ko dekhā thā.*
13.	اس لڑکے نے بات نہیں سني	*is laṛke ne bāt nahīn̲ sunī.*
14.	ھم نے سب کتابیں پائي تھیں	*ham ne sab kitáben̲ pā,ī thīn̲.*

Translate into Urdu:—

1. (The) boys have seen (the) house. 2. We have eaten (the) food. 3. (The) girls have cooked (the) bread (plur.). 4. What had (the) man done? 5. (The) boy killed (the) snake. 6. You have bitten (the) bread. 7. (The) man said this word. 8. (The) men had read one book. 9. These women have called (the) girls. 10. (The) boy gave (the) bread. 11. (The) man heard this word. 12. You had not received two bamboos.

Vocabulary.

بنانا, *banānā,* v. trans. to make, prepare, build.
مارنا, *mārnā,* ,, to strike, kill.
پڑھنا, *paṛhnā,* ,, to read.

کہانا ,	*khānā,*	v. trans.	to eat.
پکانا ,	*pakānā,*	,,	to cook.
کاٹنا ,	*kāṭnā,*	,,	to cut, bite.
بلانا ,	*bulānā,*	,,	to call.
کہنا ,	*kahnā,*	,,	to say.
کرنا ,	*karnā,*	,,	to do.
کیا ,	*kiyā,*	p. part.	of کرنا did, done.
دینا ,	*denā,*	v. tr.	to give.
دیا ,	*diyā,*	p. part. masc. of دینا , gave, given.	

(the fem. form, *dī,* is a contraction of *di, ī*).

دیکھنا ,	*dekhnā,*	v. tr.	to see.
سننا ,	*sunnā,*	,,	to hear.
پانا ,	*pānā,*	,,	to obtain, get, receive.
گھاس ,	*ghās,*	n. fem.	grass, weeds.
کھانا ,	*khānā,*	n. m.	food, dinner.
سانپ ,	*sāmp,*	,,	snake.

N.B.—*n* before a labial is pronounced *m*, as *sāmp*, snake.

بات ,	*bāt,*	n. fem.	word, thing, matter.
روٹی ,	*roṭi,*	,,	bread.
تین ,	*tín,*	adj.	three.
کیا ,	*kyā,*	pron.	what?
نہیں ,	*nahíṉ,*	adv.	no, not.

N.B.—When the negative particle نہیں *nahíṉ* is used, the auxiliary ہے , *hai,* is not necessary. Philologists say that it is compounded of *na* + *hai* = is not.

LESSON VIII.

The Genitive.

1. The relations of origin, possession, etc., are expressed in Urdu by affixing the particle کا, *kā*, to the formative of nouns, etc., کا is inflected like an adjective, to agree with the governing noun in gender and number, as :—

اُسکا گھوڑا, *us kā ghoṛā*, his horse.

اسکے گھوڑے, *us ke ghoṛe*, his horses.

اسکے گھوڑے کا, *us ke ghoṛe kā*, of his horse.

اسکے گھوڑونکا, *us ke ghoṛon kā*, of his horses.

اسکي گھوڑي, *us ki ghoṛí*, his mare.

اسکي گھوڑياں, *us kí ghoṛiyán*, his mares.

اسکي گھوڑي کا, *uskí ghoṛi kā*, of his mare.

اسکي گھوڑيوں کا, *uskí ghoṛíyon kā*, of his mares.

2. The genitive of the personal pronouns is as follows :—

Singular ميرا, *merā*, my. تيرا, *terā*, thy. اِسکا, *is kā*, or اُسکا, *us kā*, his, hers, its.

Plural همارا, *hamārā*, our. تمهارا, *tumhārā*, your. اِنکا or اُنکا, *inkā, unkā*, their.

3. The reflexive pronoun اپنا, *apnā*, takes the place of the personal pronoun when the action of the verb refers to the subject of the sentence, as وه اپني روٹي کهاتا هے, *wuh apní roṭi khātā hai*, he eats his (own) bread. On the contrary وه اُسکي روٹي کهاتا هے, *wuh uskí roṭi khātā hai*, would mean, he eats his (another person's) bread.

Exercise.

1.	میرا گھر بڑا ہے	*merā ghar baṛā hai.*
2.	میں نے اُس کا گھوڑا دیکھا ہے	*main̲ ne uskā ghoṛā dekha hai.*
3.	تم نے اُن کا گھر توڑا تھا	*tum ne unkā ghar toṛā thā.*
4.	نوکروں نے دروازے کھولے تھے	*naukaron̲ ne darwāze khole the.*
5.	اُس کے بیٹے نے دو سانپ مارے ہیں	*us ke beṭe ne do sāmp máre hain̲.*
6.	ہم یہ باتیں جانتے ہیں	*ham yih bāten̲ jānte hain̲.*
7.	عورت اپنے کپڑے پہنتی تھی	*'aurat apne kapṛe pahintí thí.*
8.	اُس آدمی کا سر بہت چھوٹا ہے	*us ádmí ká sir bahut chhoṭa hai.*
9.	اس لڑکے کے باپ نے میری جوتیاں بنائی ہیں	*is laṛke ke bāp ne merí jūtiyan̲ banáí hain̲.*
10.	تمہارا باغ چھوٹا ہے	*tumhāra bāg̲h chhoṭá hai.*
11.	وہ اپنی کتابیں پڑھتے تھے	*wuh apní kitáben̲ paṛhte the.*
12.	صاحب خط لکھتا ہے	*sāhib khaṭṭ likhtā hai.*
13.	وہ میری توپی لایا ہے	*wuh merí ṭopí lāyā hai.*
14.	بنئے نے اپنی دکان چھوڑی ہے	*baniyé ne apní dukān chhoṛi hai.*
15.	بزّاز کی دکان دور ہے	*bazzáz kí dukān dūr hai.*

Translate into Urdu :—

1. He raised his head. 2. (The) woman has opened the door of her house. 3. Your son is reading his book. 4. This boy's head is very big. 5. That man's hat is small. 6. We saw that gentleman. 7. Your letters had

arrived. 8. The shop-keepers have built their own shops. 9. He is making a large garden. 10. (The) men were putting on their clothes. 11. I know this thing. 12. They have spoken these words. 13. Cloth merchants were looking (at) cloths. 14. He made his own shoes. 15. They have seen my black horse.

VOCABULARY.

توڑنا,	*toṛnā,*	v. t.	to break.
کھولنا,	*kholnā,*	v. t.	to open.
جاننا,	*jānnā,*	v. t.	to know.
پہننا,	*pahinnā,*	v. t.	to put on (clothes).
لکھنا,	*likhnā,*	v. t.	to write.
لانا,	*lānā,*	v. int.	to bring.

(This verb being a compound of *le* bringing, and *ānā,* to come, is intransitive, meaning taking to come.)

چھوڑنا,	*chhoṛná,*	v. t.	to leave, forsake, let go.
دروازہ,	*darwāza,*	n. m.	door.
سر,	*sir* or *sar,*	n. m.	head.
جوتی,	*jūṭī,*	n. f.	shoe.
باغ,	*bāg̱,*	n. m.	garden. — باغ لگانا - to make a garden
صاحب,	*ṣáḥib,*	n. m.	gentleman, lord.
خط,	*k͟hatt,*	n. m.	letter.
دوکان,	*dūkān,*	n. f.	shop.
بنیا,	*baniyā,*	n. m.	shopkeeper, grain merchant.
بزاز,	*bazzāz,*	n. m.	draper, cloth merchant.
دور,	*dūr,*	adj.	distant.
بیٹا,	*beṭá,*	n. m.	son.
بیٹی,	*beṭí,*	n. f.	daughter.
باپ,	*báp,*	n. m.	father.
ماں,	*mán,*	n. f.	mother.
ٹوپی,	*ṭopi,*	n. f.	hat, cap.

LESSON IX.

The Imperative and the Dative.

1. The Imperative 2nd singular is identical in form with the root, the 2nd plural is formed by adding *o* to the root, as جا , *jā,* go thou, جاؤ , *jāo,* go ye.

2. The Precative or Respectful Imperative is formed by adding *iye* to the root as جائیے *já,iye* be pleased to go.

3. The 2nd singular Imperative is only used when disrespect is intended, except when used to a very near relation. The 2nd plural is used in speaking to inferiors, and occasionally when speaking to equals, but in addressing equals it is best to use the respectful form, which must always be used in speaking to superiors.

4. The particle کو is the sign of the Dative or indirect object, as well as of the direct object or Accusative of the verb. The Dative sign indicates the recipient after verbs of giving, the person on whom obligation rests, the person who has need of anything, also place to which and time at which.

5. The Precative چاهیئے *cháhiye* of the verb چاهنا *cháhná,* to wish, is used idiomatically to signify need or obligation, as, *usko kitáb chāhiye,* he needs a book (literally, for him a book is desirable or desired), and, *usko karnā cháhiye,* he ought to do so (lit. for him to do (it) is desirable or obligatory).

6. Note the idiomatic use of the verb ملنا , *milnā,* to meet. With a dative of the person concerned it means to obtain, to find, to get, as, اسکو روٹی ملی , *usko roṭí milí,* he got bread. Perhaps the distinction between *pānā* with the nominative *usne roṭí pá,í* and *milná* with the dative *usko roṭí milí* is that *pānā* implies a greater, and *milnā* a less, degree of effort in obtaining the bread.

Exercise.

1.	وھاں جاؤ - یھاں آؤ	*wahān̲ jā,o, yahān̲ á,o.*
2.	اپنے کپڑے پہنو	*apne kapṛe pahino.*
3.	بنیا اپنی دکان کو جاتا ھے	*baniyā apní dūkan ko jātā hai.*
4.	یہ کتابیں ھم کو دیجئے	*yih kitáben̲ hamko díjiye.**
5.	صاحب کو کرسی دو	*sáhib ko kursī do.*
6.	اُسکی ماں نے بچے کو دودھ پلایا ھے	*us kí mān̲ ne bachche ko dūdh pilāyā hai.*
7.	یہ گھوڑا مجھکو ملا ھے	*yih ghoṛā mujh ko milā hai.*
8.	وہ دن کو جاگتا اور رات کو سوتا ھے	*wuh din ko jágtā aur rāt ko sotá hai.*
9.	ھمارے نوکر کو دو مچھلیاں دیجئے	*hamāre naukar ko do machhliyān̲ díjiye.*
10.	اُس کو کچھہ گرم پانی چاھیئے	*us ko kuchh garm pání cháhiye.*
11.	لڑکوں کو جھوٹھہ بولنا نہیں چاھیئے	*laṛkon̲ ko jhūṭh bolnā nahín̲ cháhiye.*
12.	تم نے غریبوں کو روٹی دی ھے	*tum ne garíbon̲ ko roṭí dí hai.*
13.	میری ماں اپنے گھر (کو) گئی ھے	*merí mān̲ apne ghar ko ga,i hai.*
14.	چار لڑکے اور دو لڑکیاں مدرسہ کو جاتی ھیں	*chār laṛke aur do laṛkiyán̲ madrase ko jāté hāin̲.*
15.	ھم کو کچھہ نہیں ملتا ھے	*ham ko kuchh nahín̲ miltá hai.*

---

* See note at the end of the Vocabulary to this lesson.

Translate into Urdu:—

1. (The) man went there. 2. (The) girl came here. 3. Give my servant (a) horse. 4. We need four small books. 5. I have got a big mare. 6. Men should not tell lies. 7. She came to our house by day. 8. Leave this house at night. 9. (Please) give me four fishes. 10. (Please) give bread and clothes to (the) poor. 11. Send the boys and girls to school. 12. They got nothing. 13. (The) gentleman is putting on his clothes. 14. Give him hot bread. 15. The poor woman is *giving* her child milk *to drink*.

VOCABULARY.

پلانا,	*pilānā,*	v. t.	to cause to drink, give to drink.
ملنا,	*milnā,*	v. int.	to meet (with dat. of person), to get, obtain, find.
چاهنا,	*chāhnā,*	v. t.	to wish for.
کرسی,	*kursi,*	n. f.	chair.
دوده,	*dūdh,*	n. m.	milk.
دن,	*din,*	n. m.	day.
رات,	*rāt,*	n. f.	night.
مچهلی	*machhli*	n. f.	fish.
پانی,	*páni,*	n. m.	water.
جهوٹه,	*jhūṭh,*	n. m.	lie.
غریب,	*garíb,*	adj. and n. m.	poor, poor man.
مدرسه,	*madrasa,*	n. m.	school.
اور,	*aur,*	conj.	and.
گرم,	*garm,*	adj.	warm, hot.
چار,	*chār,*	adj.	four.
کچه,	*kuchh,*	indef. pron. and adv.	some.
کچه,	*kuchh nahín̲,*	indef. pron. and adv.	nothing.

Note.—In forming the Precative of verbs whose roots end in *í* and *e,* a euphonic *j* is inserted between the root and the affix as *píjiye,* please drink, from *píná.* When the vowel of the root is *e* this is changed to *í* as *díjiye* please to give, from *denā*. *Honā* to become and *marnā* (perfect participle *mū,ā*) form the precatives *hūjiye* and *mújiye*.

LESSON X.

The Aorist and Future Tenses.

1. The Aorist is formed from the root by adding the personal terminations.

1. Singular وں, *ūn̲*.	1. Plural یں, *en̲*.
2. ,, ے, *e*.	2. ,, و, *o*.
3. ,, ے, *e*.	3. ,, یں, *en̲*.

These are the same for both genders.

Example.

Singular.

1. میں جاوٗں,	*maīn̲ jā,ūn̲*.	(If) I go.
2. تو جاے,	*tū já,e*.	(If) thou goest.
3. وہ جاے,	*wuh jā,e*.	(If) he goes.

Plural.

1. ہم جائیں,	*ham jāen̲*.	(If) we go.
2. تم جاوٗ,	*tum jā,o*.	(If) you go.
3. وہ جائیں,	*wuh já,en̲*.	(If) they go.

2. The Future is formed from the aorist by adding گا, *gā*, if the subject of the verb is masculine singular, and گی, *gí*, if the subject is feminine singular. The plural terminations are گے, *ge*, for the masculine and گی, *gí*, for the feminine, as :—

Masculine Singular.

1. میں کرونگا, *main̲ karūn̤gā.* I will do.
2. تو کریگا, *tū karegā.* Thou wilt do.
3. وہ کریگا, *wuh karegā.* He will do.

Masculine Plural.

1. ہم کرینگے, *ham karen̤ge.* We will do.
2. تم کروگے, *tum karoge.* You will do.
3. وہ کرینگے, *wuh karen̲ge.* They will do.

1. Singular feminine. وہ کریگی, *wuh karegí,* she will do.
2. Plural feminine تم کروگی, *tum karogí,* you will do.

3. The Aorist forms have been given in this place as the Future forms are built upon them, but exercises on them are deferred to a later lesson, when the student will find them easier. In this lesson exercises are confined to the Future tense.

4. The Future suffix گا, *gā,* is a derivative from the Sanskrit root which expresses the idea of *going.* The Urdu Future وہ کریگا, *wuh karegā,* therefore corresponds to the English colloquial idiom, *he is going to do (it).*

EXERCISE.

1. وہ کھانا کھائیگا *wuh khānā khā,egā.*
2. ہم وہاں جائینگے *ham wahan̲ jáen̲ge.*
3. بچہ رات کو سوئیگا *bachchā rāt ko so,egā.*
4. وہ اپنی لڑکی کو پانی پلائیگی *wuh apní laṛkí ko pán̲í pilá,egí.*
5. صاحب کو ایک گھوڑا ملیگا *sāhib ko ek ghoṛā milegā.*
6. وہ اپنے باپ کے گھر کو جائیگا *wuh apne bāp ke ghar ko já,egá.*

7. لڑکوں کو مدرسے* بھیجو *laṛkon̲ ko madrase bhejo.*

8. هم اپنے کپڑے پہنینگے *ham apne kapṛe pahinen̲ge.*

9. وہ هم کو روٹی کھلائینگے *wuh ham ko roṭí khilāen̲ge.*

10. عورتیں اپنے اپنے بچّوں کو دیکھینگی *'auraten̲ apne apne bachchon̲ ko dekhen̲gí.*

11. وہ خط لکھیگا *wuh khaṭṭ likhegā.*

12. غریب رات کو جاگیگا *garib rāt ko jāgegā.*

13. نوکر روٹی پکائیگا *naukar roṭí pakáegá.*

14. صاحب میری بڑی کتاب دیکھیگا *sāhib merí baṛí kitáb dekhegā.*

15. بیل گھاس کھائیگا *bail ghás khāega.*

16. نوکر پانی لائینگے *naukar pání láen̲ge.*

Translate into Urdu :—

1. (The) men will eat bread. 2. (The) servants will bring water. 3. (The) boys will write letters. 4. (The) servant will put on his clothes. 5. (The) poor (man) will fall. 6. (The) horses will eat grass. 7. (The) children will be awake at night. 8. We will come at night. 9. They will go by (at) day. 10. (The) servants will *give* the horses water *to drink*. 11. She will write four letters. 12. (The) girl will cook the food. 13. Where will he go? 14. (The) flowers will bloom. 15. Fruit will fall. 16. I will see him.

See Platts on Aorist

* This may also be written مدرسه, but in either form it should be pronounced *madrase*.

LESSON XI.

The Ablative Case.

1. The ideas of separation *from*, means or instrument *with or by*, comparison *with*, time or place *from* which, are expressed in Urdu by the affix سے *se*. It is added to the formative of nouns and pronouns, as will be seen in the sentences given in the following exercise.

Exercise.

1.	وہ جمنا کے کنارے سے آیا ھے	*wuh Jumnā ke kināre se āyā hai.*
2.	وہ آگرہ سے دھلی کو جائیگا	*wuh Agre se Dehli ko jāegā.*
3.	ھم چمچے سے بھات کھاتے ھیں	*ham chamche se bhāt khāte haiṉ.*
4.	عورتیں سوئی سے کپڑے سیتی تھیں	*'auratenṉ sūí se kapṛe sītī thīṉ.*
5.	مالی کھرپی اور پھاوڑے سے زمین کھودتے ھیں	*málí khurpí aur pháwṛe se zamín khodte haiṉ.*
6.	اُستاد نے قلم سے خط لکھا تھا	*ustad ne qalam se ḳhatt līkhā thā.*
7.	میرا گھر تمہارے گھر سے چھوٹا ھے	*merā ghar tumhāre ghar se chhoṭá hai.*
8.	لڑکا اپنی ماں سے جدا ھوا ھے	*laṛkā apní māṉ se juda huā hai.*
9.	دھلی یہاں سے دور ھے	*Dehli yahāṉ se dūr hai.*
10.	کلکتے سے آگرہ کتنی دور ھے	*Kalkatte se Agrā kitnī dūr hai ?*
11.	درزی سوئی سے قمیض سیتا ھے	*darzí sūí se qamíz sítá hai.*

12. گھوڑا گدھے سے بڑا ھوتا ھے *ghoṛá gadhe se baṛā hotā hai.*

13. بنیا ترازو سے اناج تولتا ھے *baniya tarāzu se anāj taultā hai.*

14. راج مستری کرنی سے دیوار بنائیگا *ráj mistrí karní se díwár banáegá.*

15. یہ کتاب اُس کتاب سے بڑی ھے *yih kitáb us kitáb se baṛí hai.*

16. رنگریز رنگ سے کپڑا رنگتا ھے *rangrez rang se kapṛá rangátá hai.*

Translate into Urdu :—

1. She will go from Dehli to Agra. 2. (The) boys will cut their bread with (a) knife. 3. He had gone from my house to (the) bank of the Jumná. 4. (The) gardener will dig the ground with his (garden) trowel and spade. 5. How far is it from Dehli to Agra? 6. (The) gentleman will go from your house to my house. 7. Your oxen are bigger than theirs (their oxen). 8. (The) masons were building (a) wall with their trowels. 9. (The) gardener's garden-trowel is bigger than the mason's trowel. 10. He gave the poor man bread with his (own) hand. 11. Bring my shirt from the house. 12. Your child is drinking milk with (a) spoon. 13. (The) man sewed the book with (a) needle. 14. The dyer will dye my cloth with (a) red colour. 15. The boys were writing letters with (the) pen. 16. Our house is far from here.

Vocabulary.

سینا,	*síná,*	v. t.	to sew.
کھودنا,	*khodnā,*	v. t.	to dig.
ھونا,	*hoṉā.*	v. int.	to become.
تولنا,	*taulnā,*	v. t.	to weigh.
رنگنا,	*rangānā,*	v. t.	to dye.
جمنا,	*Jumná,*	n. f.	the river Jumna.

اگرہ, *Agra,* n. m. Agra.
دھلی, *Dehli,* n. m. Dehli.
کلکتہ, *Kalkatta,* n. m. Calcutta.
چمچہ, *chamcha,* }
چمچ, *chamach,* } n. m. spoon.
بھات, *bhát,* n. m. rice, (cooked).
مالی, *málí,* n. m. gardener.
کھرپی, *khurpí,* n. f. (gardener's) trowel.
کرنی, *karní,* n. f. (mason's) trowel.
پھاوڑا, *phawṛá,* n. m. spade, mattock.
قلم, *qalam,* n. m. or f. ? pen.
استاد, *ustád,* n. m. teacher.
درزی, *darzí,* n. m. tailor.
قمیض, *qamiz,* n. m. shirt.
گدھا, *gadhā,* n. m. ass, donkey.
ترازو, *tarázu,* n. m. scales.
اناج, *anáj,* n. m. grain.
مستری, *mistrí,* n. m. workman, master workman.
راج مستری, *ráj mistri,* n. m. mason.
دیوار, *díwár,* n. f. wall.
رنگریز, *rangrez,* n. m. dyer.
رنگ, *rang,* n. m. dye, colour.
جدا, *judā,* (p.) adj. }
الگ, *alag,* (h.) adj. } separate.
کتنا, *kitná,* adj. and inter. pron., how much ?
کنارا, *kinárá,* n. m. edge, bank.
سوی, *súí,* n. f. needle.
زمین, *zamín,* n. f. earth, land.

LESSON XII.

The Locative Case.

The local relations of the noun are expressed by affixing to the formative the postpositions میں, *men̲*, in, into, پر, *par*, on or upon, تک, *tak*, up to.

Exercise.

1.	وہ شہر میں گیا ہے	*wuh shahr men̲ gayā hai.*
2.	اُستاد مدرسہ میں جاتا ہے	*ustád madrase men̲ jātā hai.*
3.	اُستانی پلنگ پر سوتی ہے	*ustání palang par sotí hai.*
4.	بڑھئی لکڑی سے پلنگ بناتا تھا	*baṛha,ī lakṛí se palang banātā thá.*
5.	دو سپاھی یہاں تک آئینگے	*do sipáhí yahán̲ tak āenge.*
6.	پانچ روپیہ تک دونگا	*pān̲ch rupaye tak dūn̲gā.*
7.	ہم تین دن تک روتے تھے	*ham tín din tak rote the.*
8.	وہ ایک گھنٹے تک سوتی تھی	*wuh 'aurat ek ghanṭe tak sotí thí.*
9.	دال میں کچھہ کنکڑ ہے	*dál men̲ kuchh kankaṛ hai.*
10.	اُس گانو میں بہت آدمی رھتے تھے	*us gān̲w men̲ bahut ádmí rahte the.*
11.	اناج گدھوں پر لدا تھا	*anáj gadhon̲ par ladá thá.*
12.	وہ سوار اپنے گھوڑے پر چڑھیگا	*wuh sowar apne ghoṛe par chaṛhegā.*
13.	میرے باغ میں مالی نے پھول اور پھل لگائے ھیں	*mere bag. men̲ málí ne phūl aur phal lagāye hain̲.*

14.	اُن لڑکوں کی دواتوں میں سیاهی بهرو	*un laṛkon kí dawáton̲ men̲ siyahí bhaṛo.*
15.	صاحب کرسی پر بیٹھا هے	*sāhib kursi par baiṭhá hai.*
16.	هم نے جنگل میں ایک جانور مارا تها	*ham ne jangal men̲ ek jánwar mára thá.*

Translate into Urdu :—

1. They went from the city into the jungle. 2. We gave as much as four rupees. 3. (The) girl cried till night. 4. Four constables and two mounted (policemen) went as far as that village. 5. (The) man broke his bedstead. 6. We live in Dehli. 7. There are (small) stones on this chair. 8. They had not eaten bread for (from) two days. 9. (The) teacher took the pens and inkstand and books into the school. 10. This school-mistress has written two books. 11. The boy will read for (up to) two hours. 12. (The) child's mother was sleeping on the bed, and her child fell from the bed on (to) the ground. 13. We stayed in this house for (up to) four days. 14. (An) animal came from the jungle into the village. 15. The donkey was laden with small stones (small stones were loaded on (the) donkey). 16. (The) horsemen had mounted upon their horses.

Vocabulary.

شهر,	*shahr,*	n. m.	city.
اُستاد,	*ustád,*	n. m.	teacher.
اُستانی,	*ustání,*	n. f.	school-mistress.
پلنگ,	*palang,*	n. m.	bedstead.
بڑهئی,	*baṛhaí,*	n. m.	carpenter.
لکڑی,	*lakṛi,*	n. f.	wood.
سپاهی,	*sipáhi,*	n. m.	soldier, constable.

سوار,	*sawár,*	n. m.	rider, mounted soldier or policeman.
رپیا,	*rupiya,*	n. m.	a rupee.
رپئے,	*rupaye,*	plural	of above.
گھنٹا,	*ghanṭá,*	n. m.	bell, hour.
دال,	*dal,*	n. f.	pulse, lentils.
کنکر,	*kankaṛ,*	n. m.	pebbles or bits of brick, nodular limestone.
گانو,	*gáṉw,*	n. m.	village.
دوات,	*dawát,*	n. f.	inkstand.
سیاهی,	*siyáhí,*	n. f.	ink, blackness.
جنگل,	*jangal,*	n. m.	forest, wood, uncultivated land.
رهنا,	*rahna,*	v. int.	to stay, live.
لدنا,	*ladnā,*	v. int.	to be loaded.
بهرنا,	*bhaṛnā,*	v. t.	to fill.
پانچ,	*pāṉch,*	adj.	five.
چڑهنا,	*chaṛhna,*	v. int.	to mount upon, climb upon.
بیٹهنا,	*baiṭhnā,*	v. int.	to sit.
لگانا,	*lagáná,*	v. t.	to place, cause to touch, plant.

LESSON XIII.

The Conjunctive Participle.

1. The Conjunctive Participle is sometimes identical in form with the root of the verb as جا *jā,* but is usually formed by adding to the root the affixes کے, *ke,* کر, *kar,* or کرکے, *karke,* as جا, *já,* جاکے, *jāke,* جاکر, *jākar,* or جاکرکے, *já karke.* It is used to express the action of one or more verbs preliminary or preparatory to that of the principal

verb in the sentence, as, جاکر کہو, *jākar kaho*, = going, say, or having gone, say, or when you have gone, say, or go and say.

EXERCISE.

1.	کپڑے پہن کر باہر جاؤ	*kapṛe pahinkar bāhar jáo.*
2.	میں روٹی کھاکر آیا ھوں	*main̲ roṭí khákar āyā hūn̲.*
3.	اُس نے نوکر کو بلاکر یہاں بھیجا ھے	*usne naukar ko bulākar yahán̲ bhejá hai.*
4.	اُس نے خط لکھہ کر ڈاک میں چھوڑا تھا	*usne k̲h̲att likhkar ḍák men̲ chhoṛā thá.*
5.	اپنے استاد سے جاکر پوچھو	*apne ustád se jakar pūchho.*
6.	چور مال اُٹھاکر لے گیا	*chor mál uṭhákar le gayā.*
7.	کتابیں الماری میں رکھہ کر بند کرو	*kitāben̲ almārī men̲ rakhkar band karo.*
8.	وہ آدمی دروازہ کھول کر کیا دیکھتا ھے	*wuh ádmí darwāza kholkar kyá dekhtá hai?*
9.	ھم جنگل میں جاکر شکار کھیلینگے	*ham jangal men̲ jákar shikár khelen̲ge.*
10.	گاڑی میں گھوڑا جوت کر چلاؤ	*gāṛí men̲ ghoṛá jotkar chalāo.*
11.	کوے گھر پر بیٹھہ کر بولتے تھے	*kauwe ghar par baiṭhkar bolte the.*
12.	اُس آدمی نے چھہ روپیہ گن کر مجھکو دیا	*us admi ne chhaḥ rupaye ginkar mujhko diyá.*
13.	وہ سات پیسے کے آم خرید کر لایا ھے	*wuh sat paise ke ām k̲h̲arídkar láyá hai.*

14. بنئیے نے دو سیر دھان تول کر دیئے تھے — *baniye ne do ser dháṉ taulkar diyē thē.*

15. اُس آدمی کے ساتھہ جاکر راستہ بتاؤ — *us ádmí ke sāth jākar rásta batáo.*

16. میرا دوست دھلی میں جارھا — *merā dost Dehli meṉ jā rahā.*

Translate into Urdu :—

1. My son went and stayed in Agra. 2. My friend will eat (his) dinner and go out. 3. (The) boys went and asked (the) teacher. 4. (The) gentlemen have gone to the jungle and are hunting. 5. (The) thief, seeing the constable, went out of the house. 6. (The) servant has yoked the oxen in the cart and gone to the village. 7. Load (the) goods on (the) donkey and bring (them) here. 8. I will not go and tell him that. 9. My master has written (a) letter and sent it to Calcutta. 10. (The) baniya will weigh seven ser(s) rice and give it to me. 11. (The) master counted five pice and gave to (the) servant. 12. My mother cried when she heard this word. 13. The money (rupees) is shut in the cupboard (being placed in the cupboard is shut up). 14. He brought a letter from the post and read (it). 15. The boy came with me and showed me the way to (of) Dehli. 16. Open the door of the house and look out.

VOCABULARY.

بھیجنا,	*bhejná,*	v. t.	to send.
پوچھنا,	*pūchhnā,*	v. t.	to ask (a question).
اٹھانا,	*uṭhānā,*	v. t.	to take up, lift.
رکھنا,	*rakhnā,*	v. t.	to place, put, hold.
بند کرنا,	*band karnā,*	v. t.	to make fast, shut.
شکار کھیلنا,	*shikār khelnā,*	v. t.	to hunt, go shooting.
جوتنا,	*jotnā,*	v. t.	to yoke.

چلانا,	*chalānā,*	v. t.	to cause to go, drive.
گنّا,	*ginnā,*	v. t.	to count.
خریدنا,	*<u>kh</u>arídnā,*	v. t.	to buy.
چور,	*chor,*	n. m.	thief.
گاڑي,	*gáṛí,*	n. f.	cart, carriage.
دهان,	*dhán,*	n. m.	rice, in form of seed.
بتانا,	*batānā,*	v. t.	to show, point out, indicate.
ڈاک,	*dāk,*	n. f.	post.
مال,	*māl,*	n. m.	goods.
الماري,	*almārī,*	n. f.	cupboard, press, book-case.
کوّا,	*kauwā,*	n. m.	crow.
چهه,	*chhaḥ,*	adj.	six.
سات,	*sat,*	adj.	seven.
آم,	*ām,*	n. m.	mango.
پیسه,	*paisa,*	n. m.	pice.
سیر,	*ser,*	n. m.	a ser, about 2 lbs.
راسته,	*rāsta,*	n. m.	road, way.
دوست,	*dost,*	n. m.	friend.
باهر,	*bāhar,*	adv.	outside, out.

LESSON XIV.

The Aorist.

1. The formation of this tense has been explained in Lesson X.

2. Dr. Kellogg's name for this tense is the Contingent Future, and his summary of its uses: it "denotes a future action as conditioned or contingent" covers, *substantially*, the field of its action in modern Urdu. Other gramma-

rians have objected to the statement that this tense denotes a *future* action, and Indian grammarians and authors have claimed that "the Aorist contains in it the ideas both of the present and future." These are, however, niceties which need not be discussed at this early stage. Contingency is expressed by such conjunctions as, if, although, etc., and the use of such particles usually indicates the necessity for using this form of the verb.

3. The student will not fail to notice that the sentences in the following exercise are *balanced*. This balanced style is characteristic of the Indo-Aryan vernaculars, of which Urdu is one. In a conditional, local or temporal complex sentence the *protasis*, or clause in which the condition, place, time, etc., is stated, comes first; then follows the *apodosis*, or principal clause, introduced by its appropriate particles.

The following particles should be noticed :—

اگر, *agar*, if—تو *to* then

اگرچہ, *agarchi*, although,—تو بھي, *tau bhi*, nevertheless.

حال آنکہ, *hāl-ān-ki*, although,—تاھم, *tā ham*, nevertheless.

گو گو کہ, *go, go ki*, even if. جو, جب, *jab, jo,* if when, if—
تو, تب, *tab, to,* then.

جب تک — تب تک, *jab tak—tab tak*, until or so long—till then.

Exercise.

1. اگر بچّہ گرے تو اُس کو اُٹھاؤ *agar bachcha gire to usko uṭhá,o.*

2. اگر وہ جھوٹ بولے تو سزا پائیگا *agar wuh jhūṭh bole to saza páegá.*

3. اگر وہ بات مانے تو مُجھ سے کہو *agar wuh bát máne, to mujh se kaho.*

4. جب اُس نے دیکھا تب یہ چیز پائی *jab us ne dekhá, tab yih chiz paí.*

5.	جب وہ دیکھیں تو خوب رویں	*jab wuh dekhen, to khūb roen.*
6.	جب وہ بھوکھا ہو تو کیا کرے	*jab wuh bhúkha ho, to kyā kare?*—
7.	اگرچہ وہ نہیں چاھتا تو بھی کریگا	*agarchi wuh nahín cháhtá, taubhi karega.*
8.	اگرچہ دوا کڑوی ہو تو بھی پیؤنگا	*agarchi dawá karwí ho taubhi píūngā.*
9.	اگرچہ وہ بلاے تو بھی نہ جاؤ	*agarchi wuh buláe taubhi na jáo.*
10.	تم اِتنا کھاؤ کہ رات بھر بھوکھا نہ ہو	*tum itná kháo, ki rát bhar bhukhá na ho.*
11.	ہم کیا کھائیں - کیا پیئیں - کہاں سویں	*ham kyá khaen, kyá pien, kahán soen?*
12.	اپنے ھاتھ سابن سے اس لئے دھوؤ کہ بالکل صاف ھو جائیں	*apne hath sábun se is liye dhoo ki bilkull saf ho jáen.*
13.	اس آدمی کو پیسا دوں یا نہ دوں ؟	*is admí ko paisa dūn yá na dūn?*
14.	اگر میں اوزار مانگوں تو فوراً میرے پاس رکھو *	*agar main auzár māngūn to fauran mere pās rakho.*

Translate into Urdu:—

1. What shall I say? 2. Where shall we go? 3. When he saw the book *then* he took it up. 4. When (a) man is hungry what (can) he do? (use aorist). 5. If my horse should fall, what will you do? 6. If that gentleman calls you, go. 7. Although you should find that fruit, nevertheless do not eat it. 8. Although the medicine should be bitter, yet we will drink it. 9 Al-

though he washed his hands with water yet they remained quite dirty. 10. Shall I give this poor man a rupee, or shall I not give (it)? 11. When he washes (fut.) his clothes with water, then they will become quite clean. 12. If that boy should obey my word, then tell me at once.

Vocabulary.

سزا,	*sazá,*	n. f.	punishment.
سزا پانا,	*sázá pānā,*	v. t.	to be punished.
ماننا,	*mānnā,*	v. t.	to mind, obey.
خوب,	*khūb,*	adv.	well.
بھوکھا,	*bhúkhá,*	adj.	hungry.
دوا,	*dawá,*	n. f.	medicine.
کڑوا,	*karwá,*	adj.	bitter.
پینا,	*píná,*	v. t.	to drink.
بھر,	*bhar,*	adj. and adv.	full, complete, whole.
سابن,	*sābun,*	n. m.	soap.
بالکل,	*bi,l-kul,*	adv.	entirely, completely, altogether.
صاف	*sáf,*	adj.	clean, clear.
اوزار,	*auzár,*	n. m.	(both sing. and pl.) tool, tools.
فوراً,	*fauran,*	adv.	at once, immediately.

Note.—The doubling of the *zabar* over the alif in fauran is called in Arabic tanwin or nunation, as it shows that the *a* is to be pronounced as *an*. It marks the Arabic accusative.

LESSON XV.

The Vocative Case. The Imperative. Relative and Correlative Sentences.

1. The vocative is the formative of the noun with the nasal sign omitted, as اى لڑکے, *ai laṛke,* O boy! or اى لڑکو, *ai laṛko,* O boys!

2. There is no special form for the Imperative first and third persons. Instead of it, the Aorist forms are used.

3. The following useful series of adjectives and adverbs and pronouns should be noted:—

	Proximate Demonstrative.	Remote Demonstrative.	Interrogative.	Relative.	Correlative.
1. Time	اب, *ab*, now.		کب, *kab*, when ?	جب, *jab*, when.	تب, *tab*, then.
2. Place	یہاں, *yahán*, here.	وهاں, *wahán*, there.	کہاں, *kahān*, where ?	جہاں, *jahán*, where.	وهاں, *wahán*, there.
3. Direction	اِدهر, *idhar*, hither.	اُدهر, *udhar*, thither.	کدهر, *kidhar*, whither ?	جدهر, *jidhar*, whither.	اُدهر, *udhar*, thither.
4. Manner	یوں, *yūṉ*, thus.	ووں, *wūṉ*, so.	کیوں, *kyūṉ*, how ? why ?	جیوں, *jyūṉ*, as.	تیوں, *tyūṉ*, so.
5. Do. (adv.)	ایسے, *aise*, thus, like this.	ویسے, *waise*, so. like that.	کیسے, *kaise*, how ?	جیسے, *jaise*, as.	ویسے, *waise*, so.
6. Degree (adv.)	اِتنے, *itne*, as much.	اُتنے, *utne*, so much.	کتنے, *kitne*, how much.	جتنے, *jitne*, as much as.	اُتنے, *utne*, so much.
7. Pronoun nom.	یہه, *yih*, this.	وه, *wuh*, that.	کون, *kaun*, who ?	جو, *jo*, who (he, she, it, they).	سو, *so* or وه, *wuh*, that.
Do. formative	اِس, is.	اِس, *us*.	کس, *kis*.	جس, *jis*.	اُس, *us*.

کیا *kyā*, what ? (formative) کاهے, *káhe*.

Note again (see Lesson XIV.) that the Relative is used in the protasis and has to be balanced by the correlative in the apodosis. If Shakespeare had been writing in Urdu he would have written "who steals my purse, *he* steals trash," *jo mera batuá chori karegá wuh kúra chori karegá.*

EXERCISE.

1. جو ھو گا سو ھو گا — *jo hogā so hogā.*

2. اے لڑکو کس نے تمکو بلایا ھے ؟ — *ai larko! kis ne tumko buláyá hai?*

3. اے بھائی جو حکم تم نے دیا ھے اُس کو اُس نے مانا ھے — *ai bhái! jo hukm tum ne diyá hai, usko us ne máná hai.*

4. اب مالی باغ میں بیج بوئے اور درخت لگائے — *ab máli bág̣ men̲ bíj boe aur darakht lagáe.*

5. وہ لوگ اب گھر جائیں — *wuh log ab ghar jáen̲.*

6. جتنا دیوگے اتنا پاؤگے — *jitna deoge itná páoge.*

7. اُس نے جیسا کیا ویسا پایا — *us ne jaisá kiyá waisá páyá.*

8. جدھر دیکھتا ھوں اُدھر آسمان کو صاف دیکھتا ھوں — *jidhar dekhtá hūn̲ udhar ásmán ko sáf dekhtá hūn̲.*

7. جہاں دھان ھوتا ھے وھاں پانی کی ضرورت ھوتی ھے — *jahán̲ dhán hotá hai wahán̲ páni ki zarúrat hotí hai.*

8. جتنا تیز اُس نے اپنا گھوڑا دوڑایا اُتنا تیز اُس کے دشمن نے دوڑایا — *jitná tez usne apná ghorá dauṛáyá utná hi tez us ke dushman ne dauṛáyá.*

9. جہاں وہ جائیگا وھاں اُس کی بہن بھی جائیگی — *jahán̲ wuh jáegá wahán̲ us kí bahin bhi jáegí.*

10. جب اُستاد پوچھیگا تب اُسکو معلوم هوگا — *jab ustád púchhegá tab usko m'alúm hogá.*

11. کیا میں اپنی بیٹی کو ماروں ؟ — *kyá main̲ apní beṭí ko mārūn̲?*

12. آدمی یہاں رہے اور گھوڑا وہاں — *ādmí yahan̲ rahe aur ghorá wahán̲.*

13. وہ جیسا سنتا (ہے) ویسا کہتا ہے — *wuh jaisá suntá (hai) waisá kahtá hai.*

14. جیسا اُستاد ویسا شاگرد ہوتا ہے — *jaisá ustád waisá shagird hotá hai.*

15. جب یہ آدمی جائیگا تو وہ پھر نہ آئیگا — *jab yih ádmí jáegá to wuh phir na áegá.*

16. آؤ ہم اپنے کھیت میں گیہوں بوئیں — *áo, ham apne khet men̲ gehun̲ boen̲.*

NOTES :—No. 5—*ko* is often omitted in such locutions.
12—As *rahe* is expressed in the first part of the sentence it is not necessary to repeat it.
13 – As the auxiliary occurs in both parts of the sentence it is only necessary to write it with the last verb.

Translate into Urdu :—

1. What has been, has been. 2. Come! let us mount our horses and go to his house. 3. (The) boys obeyed the orders (words) their teacher gave (spoke). 4. He received as much as he gave. 5. Let the women cook their bread. 6. As fast as he ran so fast did his enemy run. 7. Wherever they look they see (the) sky clear. 8. Where wheat grows (becomes) much water is not necessary. 9. They speak as they hear. 10. The gardeners were sowing seed and planting trees. 11. Shall I strike my son? 12. Let the teacher read and the pupils listen. 13. He will know (it will become known) when I shall speak. 14. When the man had gone away he did not come again. 15. Boys, go and play in the garden. 16. What did I say to you?

Vocabulary.

بهائي,	*bháí,*	n. m.	brother.
بہن,	*bahin,*	n. f.	sister.
حکم,	*hukm,*	n. m.	command, order.
درخت,	*darakht,*	n. m.	tree.
بيج,	*bíj,*	n. m.	seed.
لوگ,	*log,*	n. m.	people.
آسمان,	*ásmán,*	n. m.	sky, heaven.
چانول or چاول,	*cháṉwal* or *cháwal,*	n. m.,	rice, husked for cooking.
بهات,	*bhát*	n. m.	rice, cooked.
ضرورت,	*zarūrat,*	n. f.	need, necessity.
ضرور,	*zarúr,*	adj. and adv.,	necessary, necessarily.
جلد,	*jald,*	adv.	quickly, swiftly.
دشمن,	*dushman,*	n. m.,	enemy.
شاگرد,	*shágird,*	n. m.	pupil, disciple.
کهيت,	*khet,*	n. m.	field.
گيہوں,	*gehūṉ,*	n. m.	wheat.
کيا,	*kyā,*	int. pron.	what? (introducing a question).
بونا,	*bonā,*	v. t.	to sow.
دوڑنا,	*dauṛnā,*	v. int.,	to run, gallop.
دوڑانا,	*dauṛáná,*	v. t.	to cause to run.
پوچهنا,	*púchhná,*	v. t.	to ask (a question), inquire.
مانگنا,	*māngnā,*	v. t.	to ask for (a thing), solicit.
چاهنا,	*chāhnā,*	v. t.	to wish for, desire, require.
معلوم هونا,	*má'lúm honá,*	v. int.,	to become known.

LESSON XVI.

The Infinitive and its Compounds.

Inceptive, Permissive, Acquisitive and Desiderative.

1. The Infinitive or Gerund, being a verbal noun, is capable of inflection, but in the singular only. Its Dative is used to express the purpose of the governing verb, as, وہ کھانے کو گیا ھے, *wuh khane ko gayá hai,* he has gone to eat. Instead of کو the purposive phrases کے لئے, *ke liye,* or کے واسطے, *ke wáste,* are generally used.

2. By adding to the inflected Infinitive the verb لگنا, *lagná,* an Inceptive is formed; by adding دینا, *dená,* a Permissive; by adding پانا, *páná,* an Acquisitive.

وہ رونے لگي, *wuh rone lagí,* she began to cry.
اسنے کرنے دیا, *usne karne diyá,* he allowed (him) to do (it).
وہ کرنے پایا, *wuh karne páyá,* he obtained permission to do (it), or colloquially, he got to do (it).

As the permissive is formed with the transitive verb *diyá,* it is constructed accordingly; *lagná* and *páná* are constructed as intransitive verbs.

3. Desiderative verbs can be formed by adding to the Infinitive the verb چاھنا, *cháhná.* The Infinitive can be used in the inflected form, but it is preferable to use the uninflected, as وہ کرنا چاھتا ھے, *wuh karna cháhtá hai,* he is wishing to do (it), اسنے کرنا کرنے چاھا or, *usne karná* or *karne cháhá,* he wished to do (it).

Exercise.

1. تم کو ایسا کرنا مناسب ھے — *tum ko aisá karná munásib hai.*
2. گوشت کاٹنے کے لئے چھری ضرور ھے — *gosht káṭne ke liye chhurí zarúr hai.*

3.	وہ کمرے میں سونے کو گیا ہے	*wuh kamre men̲ sone ko gayá hai.*
4.	ہم فصل دیکھنے کے واسطے کھیت کو جانے لگے	*ham fasl dekhne ke wáste khet ko jáne lage.*
5.	اُس گلی میں سپاہی نے جانے نہیں دیا	*us galí men̲ sipáhi ne jáne nahín̲ diyá.*
6.	شور اور غل کے مارے ہم سونے نہ پاتے تھے	*shor aur gul ke máre ham sone na páte the.*
7.	ایسے اُستاد کے شاگردوں کو ہوشیار ہونا چاہیئے	*aise ustád ke shagirdon̲ ko hoshyár honá cháhiye.*
8.	وہ شخص تجارت کرنے کے لئے بغداد کو گیا تھا	*wuh shak͟hs tijárat karne ke liye Bagdád ko gayá thá.*
9.	وہ ہم کو قلم سے نہیں لکھنے دیتا	*wuh ham ko qalam se nahín̲ likhne detá.*
10.	اِس مدرسہ میں شاگرد پانچ برس تک حساب سیکھنے پاینگے	*Is Madrase men̲ shagird pāṇch baras tak hisáb síkhne páen̲ge.*
11.	مُنہ ہاتھ دھونے کے لئے پانی لاؤ	*muṇh háth dhone ke līye pání láo.*
12.	دھوبی کو گھر جانے دو	*dhobí ko ghar jáne do.*
13.	دھونے کے لئے دھوبی کو کپڑے لے جانے دیجیئے	*dhone ke liye dhobi ko kapṛe lejáne dijiye.*
14.	ایسا کرنا ضرور ہے	*aisá karnā zarúṛ hai.*
15.	اُسکو چھہ روپیہ دینا پڑیگا	*usko chhaḥ rupaye dená paṛegá.*
16.	بیمار دوا پینا چاہتا ہے	*bímár dawā píná cháhtá hai.*

Translate into Urdu:—

1. It was fitting for them to do thus. 2. Trowels are necessary to masons for building walls. 3. I do not wish to sleep in (the) room. 4. They began to go to the school to read. 5. This man has come from Bagdád to Agra to trade. 6. (The) servant of such a master should be careful. 7. He went to school for three years to learn arithmetic. 8. He brought water to wash the child's face. 9. Please let the washerman go home (to (his) house). 10. You must do so. 11. I shall have to give four pice. 12. (The) policemen do not allow the men to go into this lane. 13. We began to eat (the) dinner. 14. They could not sleep for the noise and row. 15. We will go to his field to see (the) crop. 16. The servant went to cut the meat with a knife.

Vocabulary.

مناسب,	*munásib,*	adj.	fitting, proper.
هوشيار,	*ohshyár,*	adj.	careful, wise.
گوشت,	*gosht,*	n. m.	meat, flesh.
چهري,	*chhurí,*	n. f.	knife.
كمرا,	*kamrá,*	n. m.	room, chamber.
فصل,	*fasl,*	n. f.	harvest, crop.
گلی,	*galí,*	n. f.	lane.
شور و غل,	*shor o ġul,*	n.n. m.	noise and row.
کے مارے,	*ke máre,*	prep.	phrase, by reason of (lit. by the smiting of).
شخص,	*shakhs,*	n. m.	person.
تجارت,	*tijárat,*	n. f.	trade, commerce.
بغداد,	*Bagdád,*	n. m.	Bagdad.
حساب,	*hisáb,*	n. m.	arithmetic, account.
برس,	*baras,*	n. m.	year.
منه,	*munh,*	n. m.	mouth, face.
هاتهه,	*háth,*	n. m.	hand.

دھوبی ,	*dhobí,*	n. m. washerman.
بیمار ,	*bímár,*	n. m. sick man, invalid, patient.
لے جانا ,	*le-jáná,*	v. int. taking, to go, to take away.
پڑنا ,	*parná,*	v. int. to fall, to fall to the lot of, to be necessary, (with dat. of person), to have to do.
سیکھنا ,	*síkhná,*	v. t. to learn.

LESSON XVII.

COMPOUND VERBS; COMPLETIVE, POTENTIAL AND CONTINUATIVE.

1. If to the form of the conjunctive participle which is the same as the root the verb چکنا, *chukná,* is added, a completive, and by adding to the same form the verb سکنا, *sakná,* a potential compound is formed.

2. If to the same form the Perfect Participle of رهنا, *rahná,* is added the compound is called a continuative.

3. Continuatives can also be formed by adding the Imperfect Participle of رهنا to the Imperfect Participle of another verb.

Examples :—

Completive, وہ کر چکا ھے, *wuh kar chuká hai,* he has finished doing (it).

Potential, وہ کر سکتا ھے, *wuh kar saktá hai,* he can do (it).

Continuative, وہ کر رها ھے, *wuh kar rahá hai,* he is (now) in the act of doing (it).

Continuative, وہ کرتا رهتا ھے, *wuh kartá rahtá hai,* he goes on doing it.

Note.—In the form of the continuative with the conjunctive participle it will be noticed that although the form کر رہا, *kar rahá,* is that of the Present Perfect, the sense is that of the Present Imperfect; not, he has been doing it, but, he is now doing it.

4. Verbs of these classes are Intransitive in construction, whatever the first verb of the compound may happen to be.

5. The Honorific Pronoun آپ, *áp,* "Your Honour," is constructed with the 3rd person plural, as آپ کرینگے, *áp karen̲ge,* Your Honour will do (it). The words حضور, *huzúr,* جناب, *janáb,* and other titles of respect, meaning Your Honour, Your Worship, etc., are all constructed with the 3rd person plural.

EXERCISE.

1. یہ چڑیا پنجرے سے نہیں نکل سکتی — *yih chiriyá pinjre se nahín̲ nikal saktí.*
2. رنگریز آپ کی چادر گلابی رنگا سکیگا — *rangrez áp kí chádar gulábí rangá sakegá.*
3. درزی ہمارے کرتے پائے جامے سي چکا ھے — *darzí hamáre kurte, paejáme sí chuká hai.*
4. باورچی کھچڑی پکا چکا تھا — *báwarchi khichrí paká chuká thá.*
5. میرا سر دکھ رہا ھے — *merá sir dukh rahá hai.*
6. میدان میں گھوڑے دوڑ رہے ھیں — *maidán men̲ ghoṛe dauṛ rahe hain̲.*
7. دشمن کھیت چھوڑ کر بھاگ رہے تھے — *dushman khet chhoṛ kar bhág rahe the.*

8.	وہ عورت قاعدہ پڑہ چکی تھی	*wuh 'aurat qaida paṛh chuki thí.*
9.	ہم صرف و نحو پڑھنے چاھتے ھیں	*ham sarf o nahw parhne cháhte haín.*
10.	کیا آپ ھم کو اُردو اور فارسی پڑھا سکینگے	*kyá áp ham ko Urdu aur Farsí paṛhá sakenge.*
11.	حضور میں بے شک آپ کو پڑھا سکونگا	*Huzúr! maín beshakk áp ko paṛhá sakúngá.*
12.	گوالا گائے دوہ چکا ھے	*gwálá gáe duh chuká hai.*
13.	اُس بازار میں بنیا چاول بیچتا رھتا ھے	*us bázár men baniyá cháwal bechta rahtá hai.*
14.	سوار گھوڑے پر زین باندھتا رھتا تھا	*sowár ghoṛe par zín bándhtá rahtá thá.*
15.	غریب دولتمند سے بھیکھ مانگ رھا تھا	*garíb daulatmand se bhíkh máng rahá thá.*
16.	اُردو سیکھنا مُشکل ھوتا ھے	*Urdu síkhná mushkil hotá hai.*

Translate into Urdu :—

1. The boys are learning arithmetic. 2. Can the dyer dye your cloth red? 3. I have finished reading this Urdu book. 4. When the tailor had finished sewing, he went home. 5. The women's wrappers are pink. 6. Can you teach me Urdu in one year? 7. Sir! when your head aches (aor.) then please drink this medicine. 8. Let the cowherd milk the cows. 9. The girl has finished cooking the fish. 10. We will certainly learn Urdu Grammar. 11. The little boy goes on singing. 12. When the enemy left the plain and fled, the soldiers began to sing. 13. The horses were galloping on (in) the plain. 14. Let the

bird go out of the cage. 15. I have finished learning the alphabet. 16. Is it difficult to learn Persian?

Vocabulary.

چڑیا ,	*chiṛiyá,*	n. f.	bird.
پنجرا ,	*pinjrá,*	n. m.	cage.
چادر ,	*chádar,*	n. f.	sheet, wrapper.
گلابی ,	*gulábí,*	adj.	pink, rose-colour.
پائے جامہ ,	*páejáma,*	n. m.	drawers.
کرتا ,	*kurtá,*	n. m.	jacket.
باورچی ,	*báwarchí,*	n. m.	cook.
کھچڑی ,	*khichṛí,*	n. f.	a dish consisting of rice and pulse mixed.
میدان ,	*maidán,*	n. m.	plain, open field.
دشمن ,	*dushman,*	n. m.	enemy.
قیدہ ,	*qaida,*	n. m.	an alphabet or spelling-book.
صرف و نحو ,	*sarf-o-nahw,*	n. f.	grammar (lit. accidence and syntax).
فارسی ,	*fársí,*	n. f.	Persian.
حضور	*huzúr,*	n. m.	your Honour [lit. (your) Presence.]
بے شک ,	*be-shakk,*	adv.	doubtless.
دهنا ,	*duhná,*	v. t.	to milk.
زین ,	*zín,*	n. m.	saddle.
دولتمند ,	*daulatmand,*	adj. and n. m.	rich, rich man.
بهیکهه ,	*bhíkh,*	n. m.	alms.
مشکل ,	*mushkil,*	adj.	difficult.
نکلنا ,	*nikalná,*	v. int.	to go out, escape.
دکهنا ,	*dukhná,*	v. int.	to ache.
بهاگنا ,	*bhágná,*	v. int.	to flee, run away.
پڑهنا ,	*paṛhná,*	v. t.	to read, learn.
پڑهانا ,	*paṛháná,*	v. t.	to teach.

بیچنا , *bechná,* v. t. to sell.
باندھنا , *bándhná,* v. t. to bind.
بازار , *bázár,* n. m. market.

LESSON XVIII.

Compound Verbs. Frequentative and Desiderative.

1. By adding کرنا to the Perfect Participle or verbal noun in *í, á,* a Frequentative compound is formed, as وہ پڑھا کرتا ھے, *wuh paṛhá kartá hai,* he reads frequently, he is in the habit of reading.

2. In addition to the form of the Desiderative given in Lesson XVI, another Desiderative form is made by adding چاھنا, *chahná,* to the Perfect Participle, as وہ پڑھا چاھتا ھے *wuh paṛhá chahtá hai,* he wishes to read.

3. The Desiderative forms sometimes express the imminence of the action of the leading verb, as, وہ کھایا چاھتا ھے *wuh kháyá chahtá hai,* he is about to eat.

4. The form of the Perfect Participle of the verb جانا *jáná,* used in the Frequentative and Desiderative is not the common irregular form گیا, *gáyá,* but the regular form جایا *jáyá,* as وہ جایا کرتا ھے, *wuh jáyá kartá hai,* he is in the habit of going. In like manner مرا *mará,* the regular Participle of مرنا *marná,* is used in these compounds instead of the irregular موا *múá.*

Exercise.

1. سوداگر تجارت کرنے کے لئے کلکتہ کو برابر جایا کرتا ھے — *saudágar tijárat karne ke liye Kalkatte ko barábar jáyá kartá hai.*

2.	یہ بچارا ھرن مرا چاھتا ھے	*yih bechárá harin mará chahtá hai.*
3.	وہ لڑکیاں مٹھائی کھایا چاھتی ھیں	*wuh laṛkiyáṉ miṭhái kháyá chahtí haiṉ.*
4.	جب آپ کا نوکر سونے سے جاگتا ھے تب وہ اپنی عورت کو گالی دیا کرتا ھے	*jab áp ká naukar sone se jágtá hai tab wuh apní ʻaurat ko gálí diyá kartá hai.*
5.	مزدور اس جگہ پر اپنے اپنے بوجھہ کو رکھکر آرام کیا کرتے ھیں	*mazdúr is jagah par apne apne bojh ko rakhkar árám kiyá karte haiṉ.*
6.	سپاھی یہاں روز روز بندوق چلایا کرتے ھیں	*sipáhí yaháṉ roz roz bandúq chaláyá karte haiṉ.*
7.	وہ کارتوس میں بارود اور چھرا بھرا کرتے ھیں	*wuh kártús meṉ bárud aur chharra bhará karte haiṉ.*
8.	مولوی صاحب اس مسجد میں نماز پڑھا کرتے ھیں	*Maulvi Sahib is masjid meṉ namáz paṛhá karte haiṉ.*[1]
9.	صاحب جب یہاں آئے تب ھم کو بیٹھنے کی اجازت دی ھے	*Sáhib jáb yahán áe tab ham ko baiṭhne kí ijázat dí hai.*[2]
10.	پنجرے سے نکل کر چڑیا اڑنا چاھتی ھے	*pinjre se nikalkar chiṛiyá uṛná cháhtí hai.*

---

1 Maulvi being a title of honour, the verb is in the plural.
2 *Usne*, in the apodosis, is understood.

11. جب کُتّا چھوڑا جائیگا تب وہ ہرن کو دَوڑ کر پکڑیگا — *jab kutta chhoṛá jáega tab wuh harin ko dauṛkar pakaṛega.*

12. جب ہم جانے پر تھے تب آپ کے نوکرنے آکر آپکا حکم سُنایا — *jab ham jáne par the tab áp ke naukar ne ákar áp ká hukm sunáyá.*

13. اس لُغت کی کتاب کی قیمت کیا ہے ؟ — *is lugat kí kitáb kí qímat kyá hai?*

14. اس صندوق کا دام کیا ہے — *is sandúq ká dám kyá hai?*

15. وہ شام کو گیند کھیلا کرتے ہیں — *wuh shám ko gend khelá karte hain.*

16. لڑکوں کو میدان میں کھیلنے دو — *larko͟n ko maidán me͟n khelne do.*

Translate into Urdu :—

1. (The) gentlemen are in the habit of playing ball regularly in (at) the evening. 2. What is the price of these birds? 3. (The) Maulvis say their prayers in that mosque. 4. (The) dogs ran and caught (the) deer. 5. When (the) servant was asleep (use *rahná*) his wife came and abused him. 6. Let the children eat sweetmeats. 7. When (the) pupils were about leaving (upon leaving) the school, then the teacher told them your Honour's order. 8. Fill the cartridges with powder and shot (fill *into* the cartridges). 9. When the soldiers go to the plain they let off (freq.) their guns. 10. This merchant goes regularly to Dehli for trading. 11. Let the child go home, she wants to sleep. 12. The cow was at the point of death. 13. Go and give my order to the gardener. 14. When he opened the cage, (the) bird began to go out and fly. 15. The dictionary was lying on the table. 16. Put the spelling-book and the grammar-book (book of grammar) into the box.

Vocabulary.

سوداگر,	*saudágar,*	n. m.	merchant.
برابر,	*barábar,*	adv.	regularly, equally.
بے چارا,	*bechárá,*	adj.	helpless, poor.
هرن,	*harin,*	n. m.	deer, antelope.
مٹھائی,	*miṭháí,*	n. f.	sweetmeats.
گالی,	*gálí,*	n. f.	abuse, foul language.
مزدور,	*mazdúr,*	n. m.	hired labourer, coolie.
جگه,	*jagah,*	n. f.	place.
بوجه,	*bojh,*	n. m.	load, burden.
ارام,	*árám,*	n. m.	rest.
بندوق,	*bandúq,*	n. f.	gun.
کارتوس,	*kārtūs,*	n. m.	cartridge.
بارود,	*bárúd,*	n. f.	gunpowder.
چھرّا,	*chharrá,*	n. m.	shot.
مولوی,	*maulví,*	n. m.	(Mohammadan) doctor of law, learned man.
نماز,	*namáz,*	n. f.	prayer.
مسجد,	*masjid,*	n. f.	place of prayer.
اجازت,	*ijázat,*	n. f.	permission.
لغت,	*lugat,*	n. f.	dictionary.
قیمت,	*qímat,*	n. f.	price.
دام,	*dám,*	n. m.	price.
شام,	*shám,*	n. m.	evening.
گیند,	*gend,*	n. f.	ball.
صندوق,	*sandúq,*	n. m.	box, chest.
چلانا,	*chaláná,*	v. t.	to cause to go, to let off.
بھرنا,	*bharná,*	v. t.	to fill (into or with).
اُڑنا,	*uṛná,*	v. int.	to fly.
پکڑنا,	*pakaṛná,*	v. t.	to catch, to hold.

سنانا, *sunáná,* v. t. to cause to be heard.
روز روز, *roz roz,* adv. day by day.

LESSON XIX.

Compound Verbs. Intensives.

Intensive Compound Verbs are formed by adding to the root, (or rather, to the form of the Conjunctive Participle which is the same as the root) certain other verbs, as دینا, *dená,* لینا, *lená,* ڈالنا, *ḍálná,* جانا, *jáná,* etc. In some cases the action of the leading verb is intensified, in others it is so modified as to need an adverb or preposition to be added in order to express it in English. The exercises will furnish examples.

Exercise.

1. یہ دودھہ خراب ھو گیا ھے - اُس کو پھینک دو — *yih dúdh kharáb ho gayá hai, usko phenk do.*

2. اُس غافل نوکر نے پرچ پیالہ گرا دیکر توڑ ڈالے ھیں — *us gáfil naukar ne pirich piyálé girá dekar toṛ ḍále haiṇ.*

3. سوار کا گھوڑا گر پڑا اس سبب سے وہ مر گیا ھے — *sawár ka ghoṛá gir paṛá is sabab se wuh mar gayá hai.*

4. شاباش ! میرے بچّے نے سب کڑوی دوا پی لی ھے — *shábásh! mere bachche ne sab karwí dawá pí lí hai.*

5. افسوس افسوس ! کتّے ھمارا کھانا سب کھا گئے ھیں — *afsos afsos! kutte hamárá khání sab khá gae haiṇ.*

6. خبردار رهو ورنه چیل سب مُرغی کے بچوں کو مار ڈالیگی	khabardár raho warna chíl sab murgi ke bachchon ko már ḍálegí.
7. میز پلنگ کُرسی الماری سب اسباب پوچهه ڈالو	mez, palang, kursí, almárí, sab asbáb pochh ḍálo.
8. اِن مُسافروں کو بازار کا راسته بتا دیجیئے	in musáfiron ko bázár ká rasta batá dijiye.
9. مولوی صاحب ! شاگردوں کو اُنکے فرائض سمجها دیجیئے	Maulvi sáhib! shágirdon ko unke fará,iz samjhá díjiye.
10. وه لڑکی گاڑی کے نیچے دب جائیگی	wuh laṛkí gáṛí ke níche dab jáegí.
11. اگر وه دب جائے تو مر جائیگی	agar wuh dab jáe to mar jáegí.
12. اگر تم دوڑ کر اُس کو اُٹهاؤ تو کچهه نقصان نه هوگا	agar tum dauṛkar usko uṭháo to kuchh nuqsán na hogá.
13. جو مُسافر پیشاور سے آئے وه سب آج چلے گئے	jo musáfir Pesháwar se áe wuh sab áj chale gae.
14. جو کل آیا تها اُسی شخص کو بلا لیجیئے	jo kal áyá thá usí shakhs ko bulá líjiye.
15. یه سب مال اسباب میرے گهر پر پهنچا دیجیئے	yih sab mál asbáb mere ghar par pahunchá díjiye.
16. آسکے پاس جاکر یه باتیں کهه دیجیئے	uske pás jákar yih báten kah díjiye.

Translate into Urdu :—

1. Two men fell down under (a) cart and were crushed. 2. If they were crushed under (a) cart they certainly died (use intensive). 3. (The) constables ran and seized (the) thieves. 4. The patients have drunk up all their medicine. 5. The cows have eaten up all the grass. 6. The servants went into the room and wiped down all the furniture. 7. I went and told them all your Honour's words. 8. The table your Honour bought from the merchant, I have brought it to the house. 9. The person who came to-day, call him to me. 10. The travellers who came from Peshawar yesterday have gone away to-day. 11. If you cut the wheat to day there will be no loss. 12. Throw away this dirty water. 13. The teacher will explain their duties to his pupils. 14. The dogs have killed a chicken in the garden. 15. That woman will break the cups and saucers. 16. The man fell down and died.

Vocabulary.

خراب ,	*kharáb,*	adj.	bad, evil, spoilt.
غافل ,	*gáfil,*	adj.	careless.
پرچ ,	*pirich,*	n. m.	saucer.
پیالا ,	*piyálá,*	n. m.	cup.
اس سبب سے ,	*is sabab se,*		for this reason, because of this.
شاباش ,	*shabásh !*	int.	bravo! well done!
افسوس ,	*afsos !*	int.	alas!
کتا ,	*kuttá,*	n. m.	dog.
خبردار ,	*khabardár,*	adj.	careful.
ورنہ ,	*warna,*	conj.	and if not, else, otherwise.
چیل ,	*chíl,*	n. f.	kite.
مرغی ,	*murgi,*	n. f.	hen, fowl.
اسباب ,	*asbáb,*	n. m.	property, chattels, furniture.
مسافر ,	*musáfir,*	n. m.	traveller.

فرائض ,	*faraíz*,	pl. of *farz*, n. m.,	duty, obligation.
نیچے ,	*níche*,	prep. with gen.,	beneath, under.
نقصان ,	*nuqsán*,	n. m.	loss, harm, damage.
پیشاور ,	*Pesháwar*,	n. m.	Peshawar.
آج ,	*áj*,	adv.	to-day.
کل ,	*kal*,	adv.	to-morrow, yesterday.
سب ,	*sab*,	adv.	all, every.
پھینک دینا ,	*phenk dená*,	v. t.	to throw away.
گرادینا ,	*girá dená*,	v. t.	to throw down.
توڑ ڈالنا ,	*toṛ ḍálná*,	v. t.	to smash.
گرپڑنا ,	*gir paṛná*,	v. int.,	to fall down.
مرجانا ,	*mar jáná*,	v. int.	to die.
پی لینا ,	*pí lená*,	v. t.	to drink up.
کھاجانا ,	*khá jáná*,	v. int.	to eat up.
مارڈالنا ,	*már ḍálná*,	v. t.	to kill outright, slaughter.
پونچھ ڈالنا ,	*ponchh dálná*,	v. t.,	to wipe down.
بتا دینا ,	*batá dená*,	v. t.	to point out, show.
سمجھا دینا ,	*samjhá dená*,	v. t.	to explain, inculcate.
دب جانا ,	*dab jáná*,	v. int.,	to get crushed.
اُٹھانا ,	*uṭháná*,	v. t.	to raise, pick up.
چلے جانا ,	*chale jáná*,	v. inṭ.	to go away.
بلا لینا ,	*bulá lená*	v. t.	to call and bring.
پہنچا دینا ,	*pahunchá dená*,	v. t.,	to bring, cause to arrive.
کہ دینا ,	*kah dená*,	v. t.	to tell.

Note.—Intensive verbs are constructed transitively or intransitively according as the second member of the compound is transitive or intransitive.

The form *chale jáná* should be noted.

LESSON XX.

The Past Conditional and the Noun of Agency.

1. The Past Conditional, میں کرتا, *main karta*, corresponds to the English Perfect Subjunctive, as the Aorist does to the Present and Future Subjunctive. It signifies a condition which has not been fulfilled, thus preventing the consequent action etc. of the leading verb in the sentence from taking place. اگر وہ اتا تو میں جاتا, *agar wuh átá, to main játá*, if he had come (which he did not) I should have gone, (because he did not come, I did not go).

2. The student is cautioned against using this form as an Indefinite Present. Some of the older Urdu grammars have treated it as such, but not correctly. See Platt's, section 186. The English Present Indefinite, I go, I do, I say, should be rendered by the Present Imperfect, if the idea is that of continued action; or by the Frequentative, if the idea is that of habitual action.

3. The noun of agency is formed by adding the affix والا, *wálá*, to the inflected Infinitive. This is not properly a substantive, but an adjective. It is most frequently used without an accompanying substantive, but some such substantive as person, thing, is understood. If this fact is borne in mind, many of the false idioms which are frequently heard on the lips of Europeans will be avoided, such as "this *wálá*," "that *wálá*." This form has also the force of a Future Participle as وہ کل انے والا ہے, *wuh kal anewálá hai*, he is coming to-morrow.

Exercise.

1. اگر وہ آدمی یہ دوا پیتا تو وہ جیتا رهتا — *agar wuh ádmi yih dawá pitá to wuh jítá rahta.*

2. اگر تم اس سالن میں کچھ مرچا دیتے تو مزیدار هوتا — *agar tum is sálan men kuchh mirchá dete to mazadár hota.*

3.	اگر دھوبی کپڑوں میں کلف دیکر اِستری خوب لگاتا تو اچھا هوتا	*agar dhobi kapṛon̲ men̲ kalaf dekar istri k̲h̲úb lagátá to achchhá hotá.*
4.	اگر تُم هل جوت کر بیج بوتے تو تمهارے کھیت میں فصل هوتی	*agar tum hal jotkar bij bote to tumhare khet men̲ fasl hotí.*
5.	اگر تم سب روپیه خرچ نه کرتے تو اب تنگ حال نه هوتے	*agar tum sab rupaye k̲h̲arch na karte to ab tang hál na hote.*
6.	اگر بچّه روتا تو میں ضرور سُنتی	*agar bachchá rotá to main̲ zarúr suntí.*
7.	اگر بچّه روئیگا تو میں سُنونگی	*agar bachchá roegá to main̲ suṇūn̲gí.*
8.	مِحنت کرنیوالے دولتمند هوتے هیں	*mihnat karnewále daulatmand hote hain̲.*
9.	کھیلنے والے لڑکے میدان میں دَوڑتے تھے	*khelnewále laṛke maidan men̲ dauṛte the.*
10.	میرا پنکھا والا بڑا سونیوالا هے	*merá pankháwálá baṛá sonewálá hai.*
11.	دھلی کے رهنے والے اُردو زبان صاف بولتے هیں	*Delhi ke rahnewále Urdu zabán sáf bolte hain̲.*
12.	وه بڑا صاف بولنے والا هے	*wuh baṛá sáf bolnewálá hai.*
13.	کون جانیوالا هے	*kaun jánewálá hai.*
14.	اگر وه جانیوالا هوتا تو جانے دیتا	*agar wuh jánewálá hotá to jáne deta.*
15.	اگر تم پڑھنے کے وقت نهیں کھیلتے تو اب کھیلنے کے لئے جانے پاتے	*agar tum paṛhne ke waqt nahín̲ khelte to ab khelne ke liye jáne páte.*

16. اگر تم سونے کے وقت جاگتے رہوگے تو جاگنے کے وقت سونے چاہوگے *agar tum sone ke waqt jágte rahoge to jágne ke waqt sone cháhoge.*

Translate into Urdu :—

1. He is going to Agra to-morrow. 2. A tailor is a sewer of clothes. 3. Wake up, sleeper! 4. If the cook had put sugar in this rice it would have been sweet. 5. If those women had taken my medicine, they would have lived. 6. Starch and well iron those shirts. 7. If that man spend all his money, he will be in difficulties. 8. If that woman's baby had cried, she would certainly have heard (it). 9. If you had been a worker you would have become rich. 10. Those teachers are not clear speakers. 11. Dwellers in villages are not speakers of pure Urdu (do not speak Urdu clear). 12. If the boys play at sleeping time they will be sleepy (want to sleep) at play-time. 13. If you had meant to go (had been goers) he would have let you go. 14. If I had known this, I would not have spoken. 15. Put red pepper in the meat curry. 16. That man is a teller-of-the-truth.

Vocabulary.

سالن ,	*sálan,*	n. m.	curry, especially of meat or fish.
ترکاری ,	*tarkáṛí,*	n. f.	curry, especially of vegetables.
لال مرچ ,	*lálmirch,*	n. f.	red pepper.
گول مرچ ,	*golmirch,*	n. f.	round or black pepper.
مرچا ,	*mirchá,*	n. m.	red pepper or chillies.
مزہ دار ,	*mazadár,*	adj.	tasty.
کلف ,	*kalaf,*	n. m.	a kind of starch.
کانجی ,	*kánjí,*	n. f.	starch, gruel.
استری ,	*istrí,*	n. f.	smoothing iron.
خوب ,	*k͟húb,*	adj. and adv.	good, well, fine.

اچھا ,	*achchhá,*	adj.	good, well.
ہل ,	*hal,*	n. m.	plough.
ہل جوتنا ,	*hal jotna,*	v. t.	to plough.
خرچ کرنا ,	*kharch karná,*	v. t.	to spend.
تنگ حال ,	*tang-hál,*	adj.	in difficulties.
محنت ,	*mihnat,*	n. f.	labour, toil, work.
پنکھا والا ,	*pankháwalá,*	n. m.	punkah-puller.
زبان ,	*zubán,*	n. f.	tongue, language.

LESSON XXI.

Nominal Verbs.

1. Nominal Verbs are formed by combining a noun, substantive or adjective, with a verb, usually *karná* or *honá*. Some of these compounds are really phrases, but in many cases the ideas of the noun and the verb combine so as to form but one conception. Many of the nouns used are derivatives from the Arabic and Persian and are used in elevated or honorific style. In some cases, the compound, when the verb is Transitive in meaning, governs the object, in the accusative case, in other instances one of the other cases is used. The learner is recommended to note, if possible, the construction of each nominal verb as it occurs in his reading, because as in the matter of the gender of nouns, it is difficult to compile an exhaustive list. In the exercises in this book the construction of the nominal verbs used will be noted.

2. The verbs *dikháí dená* (or *paṛná*) *sunáí dená* (or *paṛná*) are in somewhat frequent use. It is therefore necessary to remember that, contrary to the general rule, the verb *dená* does not, *in these cases*, make the compound a transitive one. ایک گھر دکھای دیا, *ek ghar dekháí*

diyá, a house appeared. ایک اواز سنائی دئی, *ek áwáz sunáí dí*, a voice was heard.

EXERCISE.

1. مولوی صاحب نے نماز پڑھنا شروع کیا ہے *Maulví sáhib ne namáz paṛhná shurū' kiyá hai.*

2. شاگرد آستاد کے کلام پر غور کرتا ہے *shágird ustád ke kalám par gaur karta hai.*

3. ہم حضور سے یہ بات عرض کرتے ہیں *ham huzúr se yih bát a'rz karte hain.*

4. میں آپسے مِنّت کرتا ہوں *main áp se minnat kartá hūn.*

5. جب وہ خوفناک آواز سنائی دی تو سب آدمی بھاگ گئے *jab wuh khaufnák áwáz sunáí dí to sab ádmí bhág gáye.*

6. کُوچ کرنے کے لئے سب اسباب جمع کرو *kúch karne ke liye sab asbab jam'a karo.*

7. میرا آنا میرے نوکر کو معلوم ہوا *merá áná mere naukar ko ma'lúm huá.*

8. دریافت کرو کہ وہ کہاں گیا ہے *daryáft karo, ki wuh kahán gayá hai.*

9. فدوی کے گھر میں تشریف لے آئیے *fidwí ke ghar men tashríf le áiye.*

10. صاحب آج تشریف لے گئے *sáhib áj tashrif le gae.*

11. حضور ! تشریف رکھیئے *Huzúr ! tashríf rakhiye.*

12. یہ بات ہم نہیں بیان کر سکتے *yih bát ham nahin bayán kar sakte.*

13. اُستاد لکھنے میں مشغول ہوتے تھے *ustád likhne meṉ mashgúl hote the.*

14. خُدا نے جھوٹ بولنا منع کیا ہے *Khuda ne jhuth bolná man 'a kiyá hai.*

15. آج صاحب شہر میں داخل ہوئے ہیں *sáhib shahr meṉ dakhil hue haiṉ.*

16. ہم مولوی صاحب کی راہ دیکھ رہے ہیں *ham maulvi sáhib ki ráh dekh rahe haiṉ.*

Translate into Urdu:—

1. He began to beseech me. 2. We ought to pay attention to what our teacher says (the words of our teacher). 3. The men began to say their prayers. 4. I am making known my affairs (báteṇ) to your Honour. 5. When her father's voice was heard the girl ran into the house. 6. Go into the village which appears yonder (there). 7. The gentleman came yesterday into the house of his devoted servant. 8. We will find out. 9. This matter has become known to every man in the city. 10. The servants went and explained this matter to their master. 11. The woman forbade her daughter to cook rice to-day. 12. Maulvi Sahib! please to sit down. 13. Those gentlemen ate their food and went away. 14. The pupils are engaged in learning arithmetic. 15. The men collected their luggage and departed yesterday. 16. The Maulvi has entered the mosque.

Vocabulary.

عرض کرنا,	*'arz karná,*	v. t.	to petition, report, represent (with acc. or gen. fem).
نماز پڑھنا,	*namáz paṛhná,*	v. t.	to pray, say prayers.

شروع کرنا ,	*shuru' karná,*	v. t.	to begin (with acc.).
غور کرنا ,	*gaur karná,*	v. t.	to think upon (with *par*) meditate.
منّت کرنا ,	*minnat karná,*	v. t.	to entreat, beseech (with *se.*)
سنائی دینا ,	*sunáí dená,*	int.	to sound, cause itself to be heard.
دکھائی دینا ,	*dikháí dená,*	int.	to appear, show itself.
بھاگ جانا ,	*bhág jáná,*	v. int.	to run away.
کوچ کرنا ,	*kúch karná,*	v. t.	to set forth, depart.
دریافت کرنا ,	*daryáft karná,*	v. t.	to ascertain (with acc.).
تشریف لے جانا ,	*tashríf le jáná,*	v. int.	to go away.
تشریف لے انا ,	*tashríf le áná,*	v. int.	to come.
تشریف رکھنا ,	*tashríf rakhná,*	v. t.	to sit.
بیان کرنا ,	*bayán karná,*	v. t.	to explain, to state (with acc.).
مشغول هونا ,	*mashgúl honá,*	v. int.	to be busy in (with *men*).
منع کرنا ,	*man'a karná,*	v. t.	to forbid (with acc.).
داخل هونا ,	*dákhil honá,*	v. int.	to enter (with *men*).
راه دیکھنا ,	*ráh dekhná,*	v. t.	to look for, expect (with gen. fem.).
جھوٹھ بولنا ,	*jhúth bolná,*	v. int.	to tell lies.
کلام ,	*kalám,*	n. m.	word, saying.
اواز ,	*áwáz,*	n. f.	voice, sound.
خوف ناک ,	*khaufnák,*	adj.	terrible, awful.
فدوی ,	*fidwí,*	n. m.	devoted servant.

Note.—*Tashríf* is an Arabic factitive form, meaning *honour-conferring*. In polite language it is often used, as " please deposit your honour-conferring (presence) "= *tashríf rakhiye* for " sit down please."

LESSON XXII.

Direct Narration. Prepositions or Postpositions.

1. In Urdu the indirect narration is not used, but a statement is repeated, or a message is delivered exactly in the words of the speaker or sender of the message. Instead of saying "tell him that he must come," the Urdu speaker says, "tell him that 'you must come'"; "*us se kaho ki 'tum ko áná cháhiye,'*" اس سے کہو کہ تم کو انا چاہئے.

2. The function performed in English by prepositions is in Urdu mostly performed by certain nouns, some masculine and some feminine, used in the formative. They put the word they govern in the genitive case, the masculine if they are masculine and the feminine if they are feminine, as, گھر کے پاس, *ghar ke pás*, near the house. گھر کی طرف, *ghar kí taraf,* in the direction of the house. These are called postpositions, as, with few exceptions, they follow the nouns they govern.

Exercise.

1. اُس نوکر سے کہو کہ لڑکوں کے پاس کچھ کھانا لے جاؤ	*us naukar se kaho kí laṛkon̲ ke pás kuchh khánά le jáo.*
2. اُس نے اُستاد سے کہا کہ میرے پاس قلم دوات نہیں	*usne ustád se kahá ki mere pás qalam dawát nahín̲.*
3. صاحب نے فرمایا کہ میرے نزدیک بیٹھیئے	*sáhib ne farmáyá ki mere nazdík baiṭhiye.*
4. اُس عورت نے کہا کہ وہ لڑکی میرے سامنے کھڑی ھوکر گالی دینے لگی	*us 'aurat ne kahá ki wuh laṛkí mere sāmne khaṛí hokar gálí dene lagí.*

5	نوکر کو حکم دو کہ چولھے کے اوپر دیگچی رکھو	*naukar ko hukm do ki chúlhe ke úpar degchi rakkho.*
6.	هم کھانے کے بغیر مرجاینگے	*ham kháne ke bagair mar jáenge.*
7.	اُس نے مجھے بتایا کہ گھر میں پہنچنے کے بعد اُسکا باپ مرگیا	*usne mujhe batáyá ki ghar men pahunchne ke b'ad us ká báp mar gayá.*
8.	وہ دن کے وقت گھر کے باهر کام کرتے اور رات کو گھر کے بھیتر سوتے هیں	*wuh din ko ghar ke báhar kám karte aur rát ko ghar ke bhítar sote hain.*
9.	خدمتگار کھانے کے کمرے کے اندر جاکر میز پر چادر بچھانے لگا	*khidmatgár kháne ke kamre ke andar jákar mez par chádar bichháne lágá.*
10.	بڑھئی کو حکم دو کہ اس الماری کے موافق دوسری بناؤ	*barhaí ko hukm do ki is almári ke muwáfiq dusrí banáo.*
11.	میں نے آپ کے کہنے کے بموجب اُسکو آپ کا حکم سنایا هے	*maín ne áp ke kahne ke ba mújib usko áp ká hukm sunáyá hai.*
12.	اُسکی عِزّت میری عِزّت کے برابر هے	*uski i'zzat mere i'zzat ke barábar hai.*
13.	اپنے اُستاد کے ساتھ سب شاگرد جاتے هیں	*apne ustád ke sáth sab shágird játe hain.*
14.	مَولوی صاحب نے فرمایا کہ میں اس بھاری کام کے لائق نهیں	*Maulvi sáhib ne farmáyá ki main is bhárí kám ke láiq nahín.*

15. داروغہ نے کہا کہ میں سرکار کے حکم کے برخلاف نہیں کر سکتا — *Dárogá ne káhá ki main sarkár ke hukm ke bar-khiláf nahin kar saktá.*

16. اِس کے سِوا کوئی تدبیر نہیں معلوم ہوتی — *is ke siwá koí tadbír nahín ma'lúm hotí.*

Translate into Urdu :—

1. I have nothing to drink (near me is nothing, etc.). 2. The workman said that he had no trowel. 3. The boy was sitting near his mother. 4. His father's house is opposite our house. 5. The crow flew over the mosque. 6. How can we live without water? 7. Tell the Sub-Inspector that he must not do anything contrary to the orders of Government. 8. The lazy boy said that he was not fit for such important work. 9. The master told the servant to devise some expedient. 10. Tell the pupil that he must write according to his teacher's reading. 11. Conformably to your Honour's orders, your devoted servant has explained the matter to them. 12. All the boys went away with their fathers. 13. Tell the table servant to spread the cloth on the table. 14. He went into the dining room. 15. She came out of the house at night. 16. After cutting the bread lay the knife by me.

Vocabulary.

کے پاس,	*ke pás,*	postp.	with, by, near.
	mere pás paisa hai,		I have money (pice).
کے نزدیک,	*ke nazdík,*	postp.	near to, adjoining.
کے سامنے,	*ke sámne,*	„	in front of, facing.
کے اوپر,	*ke úpar,*	„	over.
کے بغیر,	*ke bagair,*	„	without, lacking.
کے بعد,	*ke b'ad*	„	after.
کے باهر,	*ke báhar,*	„	without, outside.

کے بھیتر ,	*ke bhítar,*	postp.	within, inside.
کے اندر ,	*ke andar,*	„	
کے موافق ,	*ke muwáfiq,*	„	according to, like.
کے بہ موجب ,	*ke ba-mújib,*	„	conformably to.
کے برابر ,	*ke barábar,*	„	equal to.
کے ساتھ ,	*ke sath,*	„	in company with.
کے لائق ,	*ke láiq,*	„	fit for, worthy of.
کے برخلاف ,	*ke barkhilaf,*	„	contrary to.
کے سوا ,	*ke siwá,*	„	except.
دوات ,	*dawát,*	n. f.	inkstand.
فرمانا ,	*farmáná,*	v. t.	to command, say, speak (honorific).
کھڑا ہونا ,	*khaṛá honá,*	v. int.	to take one's stand, be standing.
چولھا ,	*chúlhá,*	n. m.	fireplace, stove.
دیگچی ,	*degchí,*	n. f.	cooking pot.
خدمتگار ,	*khidmatgár,*	n. m.	(table) servant.
بچھانا ,	*bichháná,*	v. t.	to spread.
دوسرا ,	*dusrá,*	adj.	second, another.
عزت ,	*'izzat,*	n. f.	honour.
بھاری ,	*bhárí,*	adj.	heavy, weighty, important.
سرکار ,	*Sarkár,*	n. m.	chief, Government.
داروغہ ,	*dároga,*	n. m.	Police Inspector, or Sub-Inspector.
تدبیر ,	*tadbír,*	n. f.	plan, expedient.

LESSON XXIII.

The Passive. The Particle of Similitude.

1. The Passive is formed by adding the verb جانا *jáná*, to the Perfect Participle of the principal verb, as كتاب لكهي گئي هے, *kitáb likhí gaí hai*, the book has been written, or translating *jáná* more colloquially and literally, the book has got written. When the Passive is used, the doer of the action is very rarely mentioned. Owing to the wealth of Intransitive verbs in the language, and to the construction of the Passive Participle of Transitive verbs, there is not much use for the Passive voice in Urdu.

2. The particle سا, *sá*, which is, like the genitive sign کا, *ká*, inflected to agree with the governing noun, signifies likeness, similitude. It also signifies degree. The two uses may be thus illustrated :—

(*a*) Similitude :—گهوڑے کي سي صورت, *ghoṛe kí sí surát*, a form like a horse's.

شيرسا مرد , *sher sá mard*, a lion-like man.

(*b*) Degree of quality :—کالا سا کتّا, *kálá sá kuttá*, a blackish or very black dog.

(*c*) Degree of quantity :—بہت سے گهوڑے, *bahut se ghoṛe*, " a goodish number of horses." The adjectives and pronominals of manner as جيسا, *jaisá*, are formed with this particle.

Exercise.

1. کل بہت سی باتیں کہی گئیں *kal bahut sí báteṉ kahí gaiṉ*.

2. آج بہت سی گائیں دوهی گئیں *áj bahut sí gáeṉ duhí gáiṉ*.

3. ایک کالا سا بیل مارا گیا *ek kálá sá bail márá gayá*.

Im.- is short form of Im which is demonst. pron. denoting near at hand, + is used only c 3 words — 'imroz (this day i.e. today); imshab — this night

4.	یہ کتاب گذرے سال میں لکھی گئی	*yiḥ kitáb guzre sál men̲ likhí gaí.*
5.	ام سال اس گوری سی عورت کی شادی ہوگی	*imsál is gorí sí ʻaurat kí shádí hogí.*
6.	اسکے کمرے میں بہت سی کتابیں رکھی گئیں	*uske kamre men̲ bahut sí kitáben̲ rakkhí gain̲.*
7.	آدمی کی اولاد اس کی مانند ہوتی ہیں	*ádmí kí auḷád uskị mánind hotí hain̲.*
8.	جیسا اس سے سلوک کیا گیا تھا ویسا ہی اسنے کیا ہے	*jaisá us se sulúk kiyá gayá thá, waisáhí us ne kiyá hai.*
9.	وہ آدمی کی طرح نہیں بلکہ جانور کی طرح کھاتا ہے	*wuh ádmí kí tarah nahín balki jánwar kí tarah khátá hai.*
10.	سب چور دریا کے کنارے کی طرف بھاگ گئے ہیں	*sab chor daryá ke kináre kí taraf bhág gaye hain̲.*
11.	ان میں سے تین آدمی اب پکڑے گئے ہیں	*un men̲ se tín ádmí ab pakṛe gaye hain̲.*
12.	انکے اور پولس سپاہیوں کے درمیان بڑی سی لڑائی ہوئی تھی	*un ke aur pulís sipáhiyoṉ ke darmiyán baṛí sí laṛáí huí thí.*
13.	یہ کتابیں کسی منشی کی معرفت لکھی گئی تھیں	*yih kitáben̲ kisí munshí kí maʻrifat likhí gaí thín̲.*
14.	خدمتگار باورچی کی مدد کر رہا ہے	*k̲h̲idmatgár báwarchí kí madad kar rahá hai.*

15.	حضور کي بدولت فدوی کا مقدمہ تہ کیا گیا ہے	*huzúr ki ba-daulat fidwí ká muqaddama tah kiyá gayá hai.*
16.	بیہرا ! سب چادر تہ کرو	*behra! sab chádar tah karo.*

Translate into Urdu :—

1. This thing was said yesterday. 2. Five cows will be milked here to-morrow. 3. A whitish cow has been killed. 4. The tiger killed a whitish ox in the jungle. 5. All these books were written by (the agency of) a Munshi. 6. Tell the teacher he ought to help his pupils. 7. There was much conversation between the boy and his mother. 8. Tell the washerman to fold the clothes and sheets well. 9. By the *kind assistance* of your Honour my (your devoted one's) account has been settled. 10. The case of those thieves is not settled. 11. The Inspector came from the bank of the Jumna and told us that the thieves had been caught. 12. Just as the Maulvi behaved to us, so we have behaved to him. 13. The boy runs like a horse. 14. One of those cows is sick. 15. This year this fair girl was married. 16. Last year seven thieves were caught in the jungle.

VOCABULARY.

گزرا ,	*guzrá,*	p.part of *guzarná,*	gone, past.
امسال ,	*imsál,*	n. m.	(P.) this year.
سال ,	*sál,*	n. m.	(P.) year.
گورا ,	*gorá*	adj.	fair.

(Used with ellipsis of *ádmí,* etc. as = European.)

شادی ,	*shádí,*	n. f.	wedding festivities, wedding.
اولاد ,	*aulád,*	n. f.	descendants, children.
سلوک ,	*sulúk,*	n. m.	treatment (esp. kindly).
بلکہ ,	*balki,*	conj.	moreover, but, nay, rather.

کنارہ ,	*kinára,*	n. m.	edge, margin, bank.
دریا ,	*daryá,*	n. m.	sea, river, waters.
منشی ,	*munshi,*	n. m.	writer, secretary, teacher (esp. of Persian and Urdu).
پلس ,	*pulis,*	n. m.	police.
لڑائی ,	*laṛáí,*	n. f.	fighting, quarrelling.
مدد ,	*madad,*	n. f.	help, assistance.
بہرہ ,	*behra,*	n. m.	"bearer."
مقدّمہ ,	*muqaddama,*	n. m.	case, suit.
کی مانند ,	*kí mánind,*	postp.	like (to be) with nouns.
کی طرح ,	*kí tarah,*	,,	like (to do) with verbs.
کی طرف ,	*kí taraf,*	,,	in the direction of.
کے درمیان ,	*ke darmiyán,*	,,	between, in the midst of.
کی معرفت ,	*kí m'arifat,*	,,	by means of, by the art or skill of.
کی بدولت ,	*ki ba daulat,*	,,	by means of, by the kind offices of.
سلوک کرنا ,	*sulúk karná,*	v. t.	to behave, esp. to treat well.
تہ کرنا ,	*tah karná,*	v. t.	to settle a case, etc.
	do.		to fold, to straighten.

LESSON XXIV.

Conjunctions.

The following are the most generally used conjunctions:

1. Copulative. اور, *aur,* and; بھی, *bhí, bhí* also; و, *wa,* and نیز *níz,* also.

2. Adversative. لیکن, *lekin,* but ; پر, *par,* but ; بلکہ, *balki,* but rather, on the contrary, moreover.
3. Exceptive. مگر, *magar,* but, except, unless ; پر, *par,* but.
4. Disjunctive. یا, *yá,* or ; یاتو, *yá to——yá,* either ——or ; خواہ——خواہ, *khwáh* ; *khwáh,* whether—or (used with clauses). کیا—کیا *kyá—kyá* whether —or (used with nouns).
5. Conditional. اگر, *agar,* or ; جو, *jo,* if, نہین تو, *nahin to,* ورنہ, *warna,* if not, else, otherwise.
6. Concessive. اگرچہ, *agarchi,* although ; حال ان کہ, *hál-ánki* ; although, notwithstanding ; توبھی, *taubhi,* even then, still, yet ; تاہم, *tá-ham,* yet ; notwithstanding.
7. Causal. کہ, *ki,* because ; کیونکہ, *kyúnki,* because ; چونکہ, *chúnki,* whereas, since ; از بس کہ, *az-bas-ki,* inasmuch as.
8. Illative. تو, *to,* then ; چونان چہ, *chúnánchi,* so therefore ; پس, *pas,* hence, therefore ; پھر, *phir,* again, then, therefore.
9. Final. تاکہ, *táki,* in order that ; کہ, *ki,* that ; ایسا نہ ہو کہ, *aisá na ho ki,* lest it be, else ; مبادا, *mabádá,* lest (may it not be).

EXERCISE.

1. رات کو روشنی اور دن کو دھوپ کي آڑ چاهيئے *rát ko roshni aur din ko dhúp kí ár cháhiye.*

gen qual

2. خواہ سوتے ہو خواہ جاگتے ہو مگر یہاں رهنا چاهیئے *khwáh sote ho khwáh jagte ho maggr yahán rahná cháhiye.*

3.	ان لڑکوں کا باپ مرگیا لیکن ماں جیتي هے	*in laṛkon̲ ká báp mar gayá lekin mán̲ jítí hai.*
4.	نه آم کهاؤنگا نه سیب کهاؤنگا بلکه انگور کهاؤنگا	*na ám kháún̲gá na seb kháún̲gá balki angúr kháún̲gá.*
5.	نه صرف لکهنا بلکه لکهکر پڑهنا بهي چاهیئے	*na sirf likhná balki likh-kar paṛhná bhi cháhiye.*
6.	اُس برے لڑکے نے اپني بهن کو مارا تو هے پر چوٹ نه لگی هے	*us bure laṛke ne apní bahin ko márá to hai par choṭ na lagí hai.*
7.	شاید وهاں جانا اچّها تو هو مگر نهیں جاؤنگا	*sháyad wahán̲ jáná ach-chhá to ho magar nahín̲ jáún̲gá.*
8.	کیا گهوڑا کیا گدها بلکه کسی جانور پر لادو	*kyá ghoṛá kyá gadhá balki kisí jánwar par ládo.*
9.	کیا کرسي پر کیا پلنگ پر بلکه کسی چیز پر تشریف رکهیئے	*kyá kursí par kyá palang par balki kisí chíz par tashríf rakhiye.*
10.	گهر پر سے اُترو نهیں تو گروگے	*ghar par se utaro, nahín to giroge.*
11.	حضور اس خط کو ملاحظه کیجئے ورنه نتیجه اچّها نه هوگا	*huzûr is khatt ko muláhiza kíjiye warna natija achchá na hogá.*
12.	اگرچه اُسکا لڑکا بیمار هے تو بهی منشي حاضر هے	*agarchi uská laṛká bímár hai, taubhí munshi házir hai.*
13.	چونکه آپ نے صرف و نحو پڑها هے اس واسطے آپ اُردو میں ماهر هیں	*chún̲ki áp ne sarf o nahw paṛhí hai is wáste áp Urdu men̲ máhir hain̲.*

14. وہ نہیں آیا ہے کیونکہ اُس کے سر میں درد ہے — *wuh nahín̲ áyá hai kyún̲ki us ke sir men̲ dard hai.*

15. وہ اس لئے نہیں حاضر ہو سکتا کہ اُس کی بیوی گذر گئی — *wuh is liye nahin̲ házir ho saktá ki uskí bíwí gúzar gaí.*

16. اُسکا سارا مال اگرہ میں پڑا ہے چونانچہ وہ اُس کو یہاں لانے کے لئے گیا ہے — *uská sárá mál Agre men̲ paṛá hai, chúnánchi wuh usko yahán̲ láne ke liye gayá hai.*

17. لڑکا رونے لگا تا کہ سزا نہ پائے — *laṛká rone lagá táki sazá na páe.*

Translate into Urdu :—

1. Put these clothes on the bed and those on the chair. 2. Do not cut the bread now, but cut it when the guests arrive. 3. Whether a fowl or meat is cooked, let it be well cooked. 4. Whether the dhobi is washing or whether he is ironing yet he is not fit for work (doing labour). 5. He brought from Delhi mangoes, apples and grapes, so we all sat and ate them up. 6. The horse has (indeed) fallen down but he is not hurt. 7. Dismount from that horse or he will throw you down. 8. The gentleman read the letter because (it) was (an) important matter. 9. Learn your arithmetic lest the result be unpleasant (not good). 10. Although I have ordered (gave order of) dinner to-day yet I shall not be able to eat it. 11. You should not only learn to read and write Urdu but should also study (the) grammar. 12. Because he was proficient in Persian many men wished to read his books. 13. We came to Delhi yesterday in order that we might be present at (in) your Honour's wedding. 14. His wife died last year, but his mother is living. 15. The sky is clear therefore there is (a) good light. 16. Perhaps the man is ill, but yet he ought to be careful.

Vocabulary.

روشنی ,	*roshní,*	n. f.	light.
دهوپ ,	*dhúp,*	n. f.	sunshine.
آڑ ,	*áṛ,*	n. f.	shelter.
سیب ,	*seb* (*or sev*),	n. m.	apple.
انگور ,	*angúr,*	n. m.	grape.
برا ,	*burá,*	adj.	bad.
چوٹ ,	*choṭ,*	n. f.	hurt, wound, blow.
لادنا ,	*ládná,*	v. t.	to load.
ملاحظہ کرنا ,	*muláhaza karna,*	v. t. (with acc.),	to inspect, look at.
نتیجہ ,	*natíja,*	n. m.	issue, result.
حاضر ہونا ,	*házir honá,*	v. int.	(with loc.), to be present.
ماہر ہونا ,	*máhir honá* (*men̲*),	v. int.,	to be proficient, skilled in.
درد ,	*dard,*	n. m.	pain.
بیوی ,	*bíwí or bíbí,*	n. f.	lady, wife.
گزر جانا ,	*guzar jáná,*	v. int.,	to pass away, die.
سارا ,	*sárá,*	adj.	the all, whole.

LESSON XXV.

The Perfect and Imperfect Participles.

A thorough and exhaustive treatment of the uses of the Participles is beyond the scope of the present elementary work. The learner will, it is to be hoped, pursue his studies further under the guidance of Kempson and Platts. At the present stage all that can be done is to indicate very briefly some of the more common and obvious uses of the Participles. In the following exercise examples will be given of its use, as an adjectival and adverbial adjunct, and as a substantive. In its adverbial form the Imperfect Participle is often followed by the emphatic particle *hí*, as *dekhtehí*, at the very moment of seeing. In their adjectival form both Participles are usually constructed with *huá* the Perfect Participle of *honá*.

Exercise.

I. In these sentences the Participle indicates the condition of the (1) subject or object of the principal verb.

(*1*) *Subject*—

1. وہ آدمی بیٹھا ہوا کھا رہا ہے *wuh ádmí baiṭhá huá khá rahá hai.*

2. ہم خط لکھتے لکھتے تھک گئے ہیں *ham khatt likhte likhte thak gae haiṉ.*

3. صاحب لوگ گیند کھیلتے ہوئے دل بہلاتے ہیں *sáhib log gend khelte hue dil bahláte haiṉ.*

4. وہ ہنستا ہوا گھر میں گیا ہے *wuh hanstá huá ghar meṉ gayá hai.*

(2.) *Object*—

5. بھات پکایا ہوا طیار تھا *bhát pakáyá huá taiyár thá.*

6. دھوبی کے گدھے پر کپڑے دھوئے ہوئے لدے ہیں *dhobí ke gadhe par kapṛe dhoe hue lade haiṉ.*

7. میں نے یہ روپیہ پڑے ہوئے دیکھے ہیں *maiṉ ne yih ṛupaye paṛe hue dekhe haiṉ.*

In the following sentences the Participle is used.

II. Adverbially, qualifying the action, etc., of the principal verb.

8.	وہ ھاتھہ میں قلم لئے ھوئے کہنے لگا	*wuh háth men̲ qalam liye hue kahne lagá.*
9.	باورچی دھوبی کے ساتھہ بات چیت کرتے ھوئے گوشت کاٹ رہا تھا	*báwarchí dhobí ke sáth bátchít karte hue gosht káṭ raha thá.*
10.	وہ کپڑے پہنتے ھوئے باھر آیا	*wuh kapṛe pahinte hue báhar áyá.*
11.	لڑکیاں گاتے گاتے سیتی ھیں	*larḳiyán̲ gáte gáte sítí hain̲.*
12.	ھم چلتے چلتے دھلی کو پہنچینگے	*ham chalte chalte Dehli ko pahunchen̲ge.*
13.	داروغہ سے چور بھاگتا ھوا پکڑا گیا ھے	*dároga se chor bhágta huá pakṛá gayá hai.*
14.	رات ھوتے ھی بہرا نے بتّی بالی ھے	*rát hote hí behra ne battí bálí hai.*
15.	وہ عورت گھر میں پہنچتے ھی رونے لگی	*wuh 'aurat ghar men̲ pahun̲chte hí rone lagí.*

III. Adjectively as qualifying a noun.

16.	سوتے ھوئے کتّے کو مت جگاؤ	*sote hue kutte ko mat jagáo.*
17.	چلتی ھوئی گاڑی کے آگے نہ دوڑو ایسا نہ ھو کہ گر کر دب جاؤ	*chaltí huí gáṛí ke áge na dauṛo aisa na ho ki gir kar dab jao.*

IV. As a substantive.

18.	ڈوبتے کو تنکے کا سہارا کافی ھے	*ḍúbte ko tinke ká sahárá káfí hai.*

19. گرتے ہوئے کو مارنا خراب کام ہے *girte hue ko márná kharáb kám hai.*

20. دُکھہ میں پڑے ہوؤں کو تسلّی دینا نہایت عمدہ کام ہے *dukh men pare huon ko tasallí dená niháyat ʻumda kám hai.*

In translating the following sentences the participial construction should be used, even though an alternative construction may be possible.

Translate into Urdu :—

1. The boy was writing seated. 2. The travellers while moving along were looking at Agra. 3. The cloth merchant, telling lies, was selling clothes. 4. The thief (while) abusing the police was being punished. 5. The dogs caught the deer (while it was) fleeing. 6. He lifted the full cup and drank the water. 7. Bring the shirt ironed. 8. The shopkeeper told me this while weighing the wheat. 9. The secretary fell ill while he was writing (a) letter. 10. He began to speak (while) washing his face. 11. Continuing to read (double the participle) you will become proficient in Persian. 12. Going along the road we were looking at Agra. 13. The enemy was slain while fleeing. 14. (While) day still remained (participle with *hí*), she went to sleep. 15. The boy began to read as soon as he arrived at home (house). 16. Do not wake up a sleeping snake. 17. The child ran in front of a moving cart and was crushed. 18. Do not wake up (the) sleeping one. 19. It is an evil deed to abuse (the) dying. 20. It is a very good thing (deed) to help those who are lying ill (in illness).

VOCABULARY.

تھک جانا,	*thak jáná,*	v. int.	to get tired.
گیند کھیلنا,	*gend khelná,*	v. t.	to play ball.
دل بہلانا,	*dil bahláná,*	v. t.	to amuse oneself.
تیار,	*taiyár*	adj.	prepared, ready.

دھونا ,	*dhoná,*	v. t.	to wash.
پہنچنا ,	*pahunchná,*	v. int.	to arrive.
بتی ,	*batti,*	n. f.	wick, lamp.
بالنا ,	*bálná,*	v. t.	to light (a lamp).
اگے ,	*áge* (with ke),	postp.	before, in front of.
دوبنا ,	*dúbná,*	v. int.	to sink, drown.
سہارا ,	*sahárá,*	n. m.	aid, support, reliance.
خراب ,	*kharáb,*	adj.	bad, evil.
دکھہ ,	*dukh,*	n. m.	sorrow, pain.
تسلّی دینا ,	*tasallí dená* (with acc.)	v. t.	to comfort, cheer.
نہایت ,	*niháyat,*	adv.	exceedingly.
عمدہ ,	*'umda,*	adj.	excellent, good.
بات چیت کرنا ,	*bátchít kárná,*	v. t.	to converse.
گانا ,	*gáná,*	v. t.	to sing.
کافی ,	*káfí,*	adj. & adv.	sufficient.

LESSON XXVI.

Adverbs, and Adverbial Phrases.

Many of the expressions, by which adverbial meanings are to be rendered in Urdu, are adjectives used adverbially, nouns compounded with postpositions and phrases. As will have been learnt from Lesson XXV, many participles also are constructed adverbially.

The following is a list of useful adverbs and phrases.

1. *Time.*—(See also the Pronominals.)

آج ,	*aj,*	to-day.
کل ,	*kal,*	yesterday or to-morrow.

پرسوں ,	*parson̲,*	day before yesterday, or day after to-morrow.
ترسوں ,	*tarson̲,*	three days ago, or hence.
نرسوں ,	*narson̲,*	four days ago, or hence.
پہلے ,	*pahile,*	} before.
قبل ,	*qabl,*	
پیچھے ,	*pichhe,*	} after.
بعد ,	*b'ad,*	
سویرے ,	*sawere,*	early.
ابھی اب ,	*ab, abhí,*	} now, just now, etc. (and their cognates).
فی الحال ,	*fi-l-hál,*	
اب تک ,	*abtak, etc.,*	till now, etc.
اج کل ,	*áj kal,*	nowadays.
کبھی کبھی ,	*kabhí kabhí,*	sometimes.
کبھی نہ کبھی ,	*kabhí na kabhí,*	some time or other.
گھڑی گھڑی ,	*ghaṛí ghaṛí,*	frequently (lit. every hour).
بار بار ,	*bár, bár,*	again and again, often.
برابر ,	*barábar,*	continually, regularly.
ہمیشہ ,	*hamesha,*	always.
ہنوز ,	*hanoz,*	hitherto, yet.
دیرسے ,	*der se,*	delaying.
ہرگز نہیں ,	*hargiz nahín̲,*	never.
کبھی نہیں ,	*kabhí nahín̲,*	never.
فوراً ,	*fauran,*	} immediately.
جھٹ ,	*jhaṭ,*	
جلد ,	*jald,*	at once.
ہر روز ,	*har roz,*	} every day, daily.
روز روز ,	*roz roz,*	
آخر کار ,	*ák̲h̲ír kar,*	at last.

2. *Manner.*—Some adverbs of time can also be used as adverbs of manner (see above).

ضرور ,	*zarúr,*	necessarily, certainly.
البتہ ,	*albatta,*	decidedly.
بالکل ,	*bilkull,*	altogether, totally.
زور سے ,	*zor se,*	vigorously.
خوب ,	*khúb,*	well.
تیز ,	*tez,*	swiftly.
جدا ,	*judá,*	separately.
دھیرے ,	*dhire,*	gently.
ٹھیک سے ,	*ṭhík se,*	exactly.
مفت ,	*muft,*	gratuitously.
بے فائدہ ,	*be faida,*	vainly, uselessly.
نہایت ,	*niháyat,*	exceedingly.
تنہا ,	*tanhá,*	alone.
اکیلا ,	*akela,*	alone.
بہت ,	*bahut,*	much, many, very.
بڑا ,	*baṛá,*	as an adjective this means great, but as an adverb it means very.
صاف ,	*saf,*	clearly.

3. *Place.*—See Pronominals and Postpositions. Most postpositions of place can be used as adverbs by being constructed absolutely, i.e., without the genitive sign, as آگے, *age,* before, etc.

4. *Miscellaneous*—

ہاں ,	*háṉ,*	yes.
نہیں ,	*nahíṉ,*	no.
نہ ,	*na,*	no.

مت ,	*mat,*	not, "dont."[1]
یعنی ,	*y'aní,*	that is to say, viz.
صرف ,	*sirf,*	} only.
فقط ,	*faqat,*	

EXERCISE.

1. مہترسے کہو کہ ہال کمرے میں خوب جھاڑو دو — *mehtar se kaho ki hál kamre men̲ k̲h̲úb jhárú do.*

2. ہم نے بہرا کو حکم دیا ہے کہ کھانے کمرے اور پلنگ کمرے میں دریاں بچھاؤ — *ham ne behra ko hukm diya hai ki kháne ke kamre aur palang kamre men̲ dariyán̲ bichháo.*

3. تم نے چھوٹی حاضری طیّار کی یا نہیں — *tum ne chhoti háziri taiyár kí yá nahín̲.*

4. جی ہاں - ہم نے بہت سویرے چار صاحبوں کے لئے طیار کی ہے — *jí hán̲, ham ne bahut sawere chár sáhibon̲ ke liye taiyar kí hai.*

5. ہماری جوتیوں پر سیاہی لگاکر زور سے ملو تب وہ خوب چمکینگی — *hamári jūtiyon̲ par siyáhí lagákar zor se malo tab wuh k̲h̲úb chamken̲gí.*

6. صاحب نے بار بار حکم دیا ہے کہ ہرروز شام کو اخبار لاؤ — *sáhib ne bár bár hukm diya hai, ki har roz shám ko ak̲h̲bár láo.*

7. صاحب نے کہا تو کہا - مگر میں نے ابتک نہیں سُنا — *sáhib ne kahá to kahá magar main̲ ne abtak nahín̲ suná.*

---

[1] Used colloquially in Urdu with the 2. s. and pl. imp. in forbidding an action to be done at or near the time of speaking. Continuous prohibition is expressed by the Infinitive with *na*, as *chorí na karná* = do not steal, never steal. *Chorí mat karo* would be said to a person on the point of committing an act of theft.

8.	سائیس سے کہو کہ گھوڑے پر زین خوب کس کے باندھو	*sáis se kaho ki ghore par zín khúb kaske bándho.*
9.	آستاد نے صاف کہا کہ میں یہ کتاب ھرگز نہیں پڑھاونگا	*ustád ne sáf káha ki main yih kitáb hargiz nahín parháúngá.*
10.	وہ ھمیشہ سچ بولتا ھے	*wuh hamesha sach boltá hai.*
11.	میں نے فقط یہ کہا کہ میں یہ کام اکیلا نہیں کرونگا	*main ne faqat yih kahá ki main yih kám akela nahín karúngá.*
12.	دو برس تک یہ لڑکا اپنے ماں سے جدا رہا تھا	*do baras tak yih larka apní mán se judá rahá thá.*
13.	آپ لوگ یہاں کب تک تشریف رکھینگے	*ap log yahán kab tak tashríf rakhenge?*
14.	یہ کتابیں ھم کو مفت ملي تھیں	*yih kitáben ham ko muft milí thín.*
15.	تم کیوں دھیرے دھیرے چلتے ھو؟ جلد آؤ	*tum kyún dhíre dhíre chalte ho? jald áo.*
16.	ٹھیک سے کام کرو ایسا نہ ھو کہ تمہاري محنت بالکل بےفایدہ ھو	*ṭhík se kám karo, aisa na ho ki tumhárí mihnat bilkull befaida ho.*
17.	ھم پرسوں سویرے دھلي سے کوچ کرینگے تاکہ اُس رات کو اگرہ میں پہنچیں	*ham parson sawere Delhi se kúch karenge táki usí rát ko Agra men pahúnchen.*
18.	وہ عورت کبھي کبھي روتي اور کبھي کبھي ھنستي ھے تو	*wuh 'aurat kabhí kabhí rotí aur kabhí kabhí hanstí hai taubhí wuh*

	بھي وه برابر اپنا گھر صاف رکھتي هے	*barábar apná ghar sáf rakhtí hai.*
19.	آپ کا گھوڑا نهايت تيز چلتا هے	*áp ká ghoṛá niháyat tez chaltá hai.*
20.	وه آدمي همکو برابر دق کرتا هے	*wuh ádmí hamko barábar diqq kartá hai.*

Translate into Urdu :—

1. The boy gave the dog a good beating (beat well). 2. That man comes to our house sometimes. 3. Rouse us in the morning early in order that we may eat our *chhoṭí háziri*. 4. They arrived before we (did). 5. When the teacher punishes the boys, he punishes them well. 6. How long shall I, in vain, tell you to do your work properly? 7. He came and bothered me every day. 8. She is always sleeping. 9. I have told you again and again to polish my shoes vigorously and make them shine well. 10. The day before yesterday the constable (by) running swiftly, caught the thief. 11. The Inspector may or may not have heard, but he has not yet told me. 12. I got this bread for nothing. 13. All I said was this, that men do not work without pay. 14. He did not labour in vain because he did his work properly. 15. The master has just come, and is calling you loudly (with vigour). 16. The boys came again and again to (the) teacher and said that they could not do (the) arithmetic right. 17. Sometime or other we will set out for Calcutta. 18. Nowadays boys do not mind their father's word, as they used to do formerly (nowadays just as they used to ——— boys do not, etc.). 19. Your clothes are quite ready, sir. 20. Sometimes this boy reads well, but sometimes he is very lazy.

Vocabulary.

هال کمره ,	*hál kamra,*	n. m.	drawing-room.
جھاڑو ,	*jháṛū,*	n. m.	broom.

جھاڑو دینا ,	*jhárū dená,*	v. t.	to sweep.
مہتر ,	*mihtár,*	n. m.	sweeper.

The word is a title of honour, applied as a euphemism to the "knight of the broom."

دری ,	*darí,*	n. f.	carpet (made of cotton).
حاضری ,	*háziri,*	n. f.	breakfast.
چھوٹی ,	*chhoṭí háziri,*	n. f.	early or "little" breakfast.
سیاھی ,	*siyáhí,*	n. f.	blacking, or ink.
ملنا ,	*malná,*	v. t.	to rub.
چمکنا ,	*chamakná,*	v. int.	to shine.
اخبار ,	*akhbár,*	n. m.	news, newspaper.
زین ,	*zín,*	n. m.	saddle.
کسنا ,	*kasná,*	v. t.	to tighten, bind.
سائس ,	*sáis,*	n. m.	groom.
سچ بولنا ,	*sach bolná,*	v. int.,	to tell the truth.
دق کرنا ,	*diqq karná,*	v. t.	to annoy.

LESSON XXVII.

NUMERALS.

1. ایک , *ek.*
2. دو , *do.*
3. تین , *tín.*
4. چار , *chár.*
5. پانچ , *pāṉch.*
6. چھه , *chha.*
7. سات , *sát.*
8. آٹھه , *áṭh.*
9. نو , *nau.*
10. دس , *das.*
11. گیارہ , *gyárah.*
12. بارہ , *bárah.*
13. تیرہ , *terah.*
14. چودہ , *chaudah.*

15. پندره, *pandrah.*
16. سوله, *solah.*
17. سترہ, *sattrah.*
18. اٹھاره, *aṭhára.*
19. اُنیس, *unís.*
20. بیس, *bis.*
21. اکیس, *ekís.*
22. بائیس, *báís.*
23. تیئس, *teís.*
24. چوبیس, *chaubís.*
25. پچیس, *pachís.*
26. چھبیس, *chhabbís.*
27. ستائیس, *satáís.*
28. اٹھائیس, *aṭháís.*
29. اُنتیس, *untís.*
30. تیس, *tís.*
31. اکتیس, *ektís.*
32. بتیس, *batís.*
33. تینتیس, *teṉtís.*
34. چونتیس, *chauṉtís.*
35. پینتیس, *paintís.*
36. چھتیس, *chhattís.*
37. سینتیس, *saiṉtís.*
38. اڑتیس, *aṛtís.*
39. اُنچالیس, *untálís.*
40. چالیس, *chálís.*
41. اکتالیس, *ektálís.*
42. بیالیس, *bayális.*
43. تینتالیس, *teṉtális.*
44. چوالیس, *chauális.*
45. پینتالیس, *paiṉtális.*
46. چھیالیس, *chhiyális.*
47. سینتالیس, *saiṉtalís.*
48. اڑتالیس, *aṛtális.*
49. اُنچاس, *unchás.*
50. پچاس, *pachás.*
51. اکیاون, *ikáwán.*
52. باون, *báwan.*
53. ترپن, *tirpan.*
54. چوون, *chauwan.*
55. پچپن, *pachpan.*
56. چھپن, *chhappan.*
57. ستاون, *satáw̱an.*
58. اٹھاون, *aṭháwan.*
59. اُنسٹھ, *unsaṭh.*
60. ساٹھ, *sáṭh.*
61. اکسٹھ, *iksaṭh.*
62. باسٹھ, *básaṭh.*
63. ترسٹھ, *tirsaṭh.*
64. چونسٹھ, *chauṉsath.*
65. پینسٹھ, *painsaṭh.*
66. چھیاسٹھ, *chhiyásath.*
67. سڑسٹھ, *saṛsaṭh.*
68. اڑسٹھ, *aṛsath.*
69. اُنہتر, *unhattar.*
70. ستر, *sattar.*
71. اکہتر, *ikhattar.*
72. بہتر, *bahattar.*
73. تہتر, *tihattar.*
74. چوہتر, *chauhattar.*

75. پچھتر, *pachhattar.*
76. چھہتر, *chhahattar.*
77. ستہتر, *sathattar.*
78. اٹھتر, *aṭhattar.*
79. اُناسی, *unásí.*
80. اسی, *assi.*
81. اکاسی, *ikásí.*
82. بیاسی, *biyásí.*
83. تراسی, *tirásí.*
84. چوراسی, *chaurásí.*
85. پچاسی, *pachásí.*
86. چھیاسی, *chhiyási.*
87. ستاسی, *satásí.*
88. اٹھاسی, *aṭhásí.*
89. نواسی, *nauásí.*
90. نوے, *nawwe.*
91. اکانوے, *ekánwe.*
92. بانوے, *bánwe.*
93. ترانوے, *tiránwe.*
94. چورانوے, *chauránwe.*
95. پچانوے, *pachánawe.*
96. چھیانوے, *chhiyánawe.*
97. ستانوے, *satanáwe.*
98. اٹھانوے, *aṭhánawe.*
99. ننانوے, *ninánawe.*
100. سو, *sau.*

The ordinals are formed by adding *wáṉ* or *wíṉ* (masc. or fem.) as the case may be, except in the case of the first four, and the sixth.

پہلا, *pahilá* (*le, li*), first, دوسرا, *dúsrá*, second, تیسرا, *tísrá*, third, چوتھا, *chauthá*, fourth, پانچواں, *panchwán*, fifth, چھٹواں, *chhaṭhwán*, sixth, ساتواں, *sátwán*, seventh, and so on. ہزار, *hazár*, one thousand, لاکھ, *lákh*, a hundred thousand, کروڑ, *karoṛ*, ten millions.

The following fractionals are in constant use :—

چوتھا, *chauthá*, a fourth.

پونے, *paune*, a quarter less; as, *paune do*, $1\frac{3}{4}$.

سوا, *sawa*, a quarter more; as, *sawa tín*, $3\frac{1}{4}$.

ڈیڑھ, *deṛh*, one and a half, اڑھائی or ڈھائی, *aṛhái* or *ḍhái* two and a half.

ساڑھے, *sáṛhe*, a half more, as, *sáṛhe chár*, $4\frac{1}{2}$.

گنا, *guná* when added to a number means "fold" as *do guná*, two-fold.

Exercise.

1.	لڑکیاں دو سوئیاں چاہتی تھیں	*laṛkiyán do súíyán cháhtí thin.*
2.	ہم نے اسکے لئے ڈیڑھ پیسہ دیے ہیں	*ham ne is ke liye ḍeṛh paisa diyá hain.*
3.	اس کی قیمت پچاس روپیہ ہے	*uskí qímat pachás rupaye hai.*
4.	دو آنے کے بوتام خریدو	*do áne ke botám kharído.*
5.	ڈیڑھ سیر چاول - دو سیر گھی اور آدھا سیر نمک چاہئے	*ḍeṛh ser cháwal, do ser ghí aur ádhá ser namak cháhiye.*
6.	تین بجے کو آئیے	*tín baje ko áiye.*
7.	وہ ڈیڑھ بجے کو گیا	*wuh ḍeṛh baje ko gayá.*
8.	کل ہم پانچ بجے اٹھینگے	*kal ham pánch baje uṭhenge.*
9.	وہ دو پہر تک اٹھیگا	*wuh do pahaṛ tak uṭhegá.*
10.	صاحب آدھی رات کے قبل تشریف لائینگے	*sáhib ádhí rát ke qabl tashríf láenge.*
11.	گھوڑے کے واسطے دو من چنا منگاؤ	*ghoṛe ke wáste do man chaná mangáo.*
12.	ہم تین بجے کے بعد جائینگے	*ham tín baje ke b'ad jáenge.*
13.	لڑکے ساڑھے چار بجے کو چھٹی پائینگے	*laṛke sáṛhe chár baje ko chhuṭṭi p'aenge.*
14.	دو پیپے تیل ہمارے گھر کو بھیجو	*do pípe tel hamáre ghar ko bhejo.*

15. بارہ قمیص - دو درزن کالر چھہ گلابند - چار رات کے جوڑے نو جوڑے موزے - چوبیس رومال - چار کوٹ بیس بنیائین - چار واسکٹ چار پتلون - چار کمربند یہ سب گن کر صندوق میں تہ کر کے رکھو

bárah qamíz, do darzan kálar, chhah galaband, chár rát ke jore, nau jore moze, chaubís rumál, chár koṭ, bís banyán, chár wáskit, chár patlún, chár kamarband ; yih sab ginkar sandúq meṉ tah karke rakho.

16. میں پہلے دفعہ کو معاف کرونگا لیکن پھر نہیں کرونگا

maiṉ pahile dafá ko mu'áf karúṉga, lekin phir nahíṉ karúṉga.

Translate into Urdu :—

1. Give the *darzi* twelve buttons. 2. Order a dozen shirts, six (pairs of) trousers, six coats and six handkerchiefs. 3. Tell the *dhobi* to bring my night suits and two pairs of socks quickly. 4. Give me a ser and a half of rice and three quarters of a ser of salt. 5. Buy four maunds of gram for the horse. 6. Send them not later than (up to) six o'clock. 7. You do not need half a ser of ghi to cook to-day's dinner. 8. Bring five sers and a half of milk for the school-boys. 9. I sell twenty-four mangoes for the (one) rupee. 10. The Maulvi went to say prayers at 5 o'clock in the (at) evening. 11. He will not reach the mosque before half-past one. 12. They arrived after half past-two. 13. I have not two tins of oil in (the) shop (in shop are not, etc.) 14. Bring two rupees worth of grapes (grapes of two rupees). 15. Yesterday that lazy man did not wake till eight o'clock. 16. I will go to his house the first time, but after that he must come to me.

VOCABULARY.

بوتام ,	*botam,*	n. m.	button.
گھی ,	*ghí,*	n. m.	clarified butter.

نمک ,	*namak,*	n. m.	salt.
بجا بجے ,	*bajá, baje,*	p. part. adverbially used of *bajná* to strike — o'clock.	
دوپہر ,	*do pahar,*	n. m.	noon.

Pahar means a watch of 3 hours, noon is the 2nd watch of the day and midnight of the night.

ادھی رات ,	*adhi rát,*	lit. half night, midnight.	
من ,	*man,*	n. m.	40 sers.
دفع ,	*dafá,*	n. m.	time, turn.
چنا ,	*chaná,*	n. m.	gram, chick pea.
منگانا ,	*mangáná,*	v. t.	to order.
چھٹی ,	*chuṭṭhi,*	n. f.	leave, holiday, release.
پیپہ ,	*pípá,*	n. m.	tin, barrel.
درزن ,	"*darzan,*"	n. m.	a dozen.
کالر ,	*kálar,*	n. m.	collar.
گلہ بند ,	*galaband,*	n. m.	necktie.
رومال ,	*rúmál,*	n. m.	handkerchief.
جوڑہ ,	*joṛa,*	n. m.	suit of clothes, a pair.
موزہ ,	*moza,*	n. m.	sock, stocking.
بنیان ,	*banyán,*	n. m.	undervest.
واسکٹ ,	"*wáskit,*"	n. f.(?)	waistcoat.
پتلون ,	"*patlún,*"	n. m.	pantaloons, trousers.
کمربند ,	*kamarband,*	n. m.	sash.
معاف کرنا ,	*muáf karná,*	v. t.	to forgive.

———

LESSON XXVIII.

Presumptive and Conditional Forms.

By adding the Aorist, Future, or Present forms of the verb *honá*, to become, to the Imperfect and Perfect Participles of the verb, three pairs of tenses can be formed, all of them conveying the ideas of contingency, presumption or potentiality. Each grammarian seems to have a special name for each of these tenses. Dr. Kellogg's nomenclature is the most luminous and logical, Mr. Platts's is careful and laborious, but does not label these tenses as contingent, and Mr. Kempson's translates strictly the nomenclature of the indigenous grammarians. We give Kempson's, with Kellogg's in brackets.

1. Present Dubious, (Contingent Imperfect), وہ آتا ہو, *wuh átá ho,* he may be coming.

2. Past Dubious, (Contingent Perfect), وہ آیا ہو, *wuh áyá ho,* he may have come.

3. Present Presumptive, (Presumptive Imperfect), وہ آتا ہوگا, *wuh átá hoga,* he will, or must be coming.

4. Past Presumptive, (Presumptive Perfect), وہ آیا ہوگا, *wuh áyá hogá,* he will, or must have come.

5. Past Conditional, (Past Contingent Imperfect), وہ آتا ہوتا, *wuh átá hotá,* had he been coming.

6. Past Conditional, (Remote) (Past Contingent Perfect), وہ آیا ہوتا, had he (not) come.

No. 1. "If Mohan be on the way here we may see him to-day"; he may be coming, but of this we cannot be sure.

No. 2. "If Mohan has arrived here we might see him to-night"; he may have arrived, but of this we are ignorant.

No. 3. (Mohan promised to come, therefore) "he will be on the way here," so we may expect to see him to-night.

No. 4. (Mohan was to arrive this afternoon therefore) "he will have come," so let us go and see him.

No. 5. "Had Mohan been (on the road) coming, we should (be able to) see him on the road." He is not coming therefore we do not see him.

No. 6. "Had Mohan arrived we could have seen him." He had not arrived so we could not see him.

Exercise.

1.	اگر باورچی کھانا پکاتا هو تو هم آٹهه بجے کھانے پائینگے	*agar báwarchí kháná pakátá ho, to ham áṭh baje khâne páen̲ge.*
2.	اگر مہتر نے جھاڑو دیا هو تو هم هال کمرے میں بیٹهه سکینگے	*agar mehtar ne jhárú diyá ho, to ham hál kamre men̲ baiṭh saken̲ge.*
3.	شاید لڑکے پڑھتے هوں	*sháyad laṛke paṛhte hon̲.*
4.	شاید مالک نے نوکر کو حکم دیا هو	*sháyad malik ne naukar ko hukm diyá ho.*
5.	اب گوالا گائے کو دُهتا هوگا جاکر دیکھو که وه پاني نه ملائے	*ab gwálá gáe ko duhtá hogá jákaṛ dekho ki wuh pání na miláe.*
6.	مولوي صاحب مسجد سے آے هونگے - آؤ هم جاکر اُس سے دریافت کریں	*Maulví sáhib masjid se áye hon̲gé, áo ham jákar us se daryáft káren̲.*
7.	تمهارا باپ کہتا هوگا - جا دیکھو	*tumhárá báp khátá hogá já dekho.*
8.	اب بچّه سو گیا هوگا - کیونکه اُس کي آواز نہیں سنائی دیتی	*ab bachcha so gaya hogá kyún̲ki us kí áwaz nahín̲ sunáí detí.*

9.	اگر نوکر جھاڑ پونچھہ کرتا ھوتا تو وہ گھر کے باھر نہ پایا جاتا	*agar naukar jháṛ ponchh kartá hota to wuh ghar ke báhar na payá játá.*
10.	اگر اس لڑکے نے گالی دی نہ ھوتی تو وہ نہیں مارا جاتا	*agar is laṛke ne gálí dí na hotí to wuh nahín márá játá.*
11.	بعض نوکر بیھرا - بعض مہتر بعض باورچی اور بعض سائیس کہلاتے ھین	*báz naukaṛ behra, báz mehtar, báz bawarchi aur báz sáís kahláte hain.*
12.	اگر دس ھی انڈے پکاؤ تو کافی ھونگے	*agar das hí aṇḍe pakáo to káfí honge.*
13.	گھاس ھري یا سبز ھوتی ھے - مگر یہ گھاس نہیں ھوگا کیونکہ یہ بالکل کالا ھے	*ghás harí yá sabz hoti hai magar yih ghás nahin hai kyúnki yih bilkull kálá hai.*
14.	دھوبی کو کچھہ سابن دو اور اُس کو تاکید کرکے کہو کہ پھر اپنا کام ادھورا نہ چھوڑے	*dhobí ko kuchh sábun do aur us ko tákíd karke kaho ki phir apná kam adhúrá na chhoṛe.*
15.	صاحب یہ مُمکن نہیں کہ میں آپ سے جُھوٹ بات کہوں	*sáhib, yih mumkin nahín ki main áp se jhúṭh bát kahún.*
16.	گائے کو باغ سے نکالو نہیں تو وہ گھاس کے علاوہ سب پھول چریگی	*gáe ko bágh se nikálo nahin to wuh ghás ke 'aláwa sab phúl charegí.*
17.	چھوٹی چھوٹی چڑیاں سڑک پر دانہ چُگ رہی ھیں	*chhoṭí chhoṭí chiṛiyán saṛak par dáná chug rahí hain.*
18.	آپ کا کہنا درست ھے	*áp ká kahná durust hai.*

19. ہوشیاری کے ساتھ لکھنا واجب ہے *hoshyárí ke sáth likhná wájib hai.*

20. میں لکھہ چکا ہوں اب آداب عرض کرتا ہوں *main̲ likh chuká hún̲ ab ádáb ʻarz kartá hún̲.*

Translate into Urdu :—

1. If the master is now writing a letter, you will have to take it to the post. 2. If the table servant has laid the cloth we shall soon have (eat) the dinner. 3. Perhaps he may be telling the truth. 4. Has the boy not arrived? look, he may have fallen into the river. 5. The cow will just now be grazing in the garden, go and catch her. 6. The gentleman will have read Persian, that is why (for this reason) he is proficient in Urdu. 7. The tailor will be making (sewing) my trousers, tell him to bring them quickly. 8. The girl will have fallen off the chair, for she is crying. 9. If you had been wishful (wishing) to hear my order, you would certainly have heard. 10. If the thief had not stolen the grain he would not have been seized and punished. 11. Some people laugh, some cry, and some neither laugh nor cry. 12. If the *dhobi* will bring only one shirt that will be enough. 13. This is not a mango because it is red and mangoes are green or yellow. 14. Insist on the boys reading Persian. 15. That is a bad servant, who leaves his work half done. 16. Besides bread give the poor man some fish. 17. The little birds will peck up the wheat. 18. The ox is grazing in the jungle. 19. Before I finish writing I will make my parting salutation. 20. It is fitting that you write this carefully.

VOCABULARY.

دریافت کرنا,	*daryáft karná,*	v. t.	to ascertain.
کہلانا,	*kahlána,*	v. int.	to be called.
ملانا,	*miláná,*	v. t.	to mix.

بعض ,	*b'az,*	indef.	adj. and pron. some.
انڈا ,	*andá,*	n. m.	egg.
کافی ,	*káfí,*	adj.	enough, sufficient.
تاکید کرنا ,	*takíd karná,*	v. t.	to insist.
ادھورا ,	*adhúrá,*	adj.	half done, half and half.
ممکن ,	*mumkin,*	adj.	possible.
کے علاوہ ,	*ke 'aláwa,*	postp.	in addition to, besides.
جھاڑ پونچھہ کرنا ,	*jhár ponchh karná,*		to dust a room.
چرنا ,	*charná,*	v. int.	to graze.
چگنا ,	*chugná,*	v. t.	to pick up food with the beak, to peck.
سڑک ,	*saṛak,*	n. f.	roadway, road.
دانا ,	*dáná,*	n. m.	grain.
درست ,	*durust,*	adj.	straight, correct.
هوشیاری ,	*hoshiyárí,*	n. f.	carefulness, vigilance.
واجب ,	*wájib,*	adj.	fitting, proper.
اداب عرض کرنا ,	*ádáb a'rz karná,*		to make a parting salutation.

The Urdu Noun and Pronoun.

		Masculine in ā.	Masculine in consonant.	Feminine in ī.	Feminine in consonant.	Pronoun, 1st Person.
Nom.	S.	گھوڑا , *ghoṛá*	بیل , *bail*	بیوي , *bíwí*	رات *rát*	میں , *maiṉ.*
Agent.	S.	گھوڑے نے, *ghoṛe ne*	بیل نے, *bail ne*	بیوي نے, *bíwí ne*	راتنے , *rát ne*	میں نے, *maiṉ ne*
Formative	S.	گھوڑے , *ghoṛe*	بیل , *bail*	بیوي , *bíwí*	رات , *rát*	مجھه , *mujh.*
or (Gen.)	S.	,, ,,	,, ,,	,, ,,	رات , *rát*	میرا , *mera.*
Nom.	P.	گھوڑے , *ghoṛe*	بیل , *bail*	بیویاں , *bíwíyáṉ*	راتیں, *ráteṉ*	هم , *ham.*
Ag. and Formative	P.	گھوڑوں , *ghoṛoṉ*	بیلوں , *bailoṉ*	بیویوں , *bíwíyoṉ*	راتوں, *rátoṉ*	هم , *ham.*
Gen.	P.	,, ,,	,, ,,	,, ,,	,, ,,	همارا , *hamárá*

The Urdu Verb.

Root,	بول,	*bol.*
Infinitive,	بولنا ,	*bolná.*
Conjunctive Participle,	بولکے بولکر ,	*bolke, bolkar.*
Imperfect ,,	بولتا ,	*boltá.*
Perfect ,,	بولا ,	*bolá.*
Noun of Agency,	بولنے والا ,	*bolnewálá.*

Tenses from the root (3rd pers. sing.).

Aorist,	بولے ,	*bole.*
Imperative (2nd pers. pl.)	بولو ,	*bolo.*
Future (3rd pers. sing.)	بولیگا	*bolegá.*

Tenses from the Imperfect Participle (3rd pers. sing.).

Past Conditional,	بولتا ,	*boltá.*
Present Imperfect,	بولتا هے ,	*boltá hai.*
Past Imperfect,	بولتا تها ,	*boltá thá.*
Present Dubious, ~~Future~~ perfect	بولتا هو ,	*boltá ho.*
,, Presumptive,	بولتا هوگا ,	*boltá hogá.*
Past Conditional or Optative, 2nd form,	بولتا هوتا ,	*boltá hotá.*

Tenses from the Perfect Participle (3rd pers. sing.).

Past Absolute or Indefinite,	بولا ,	*bolá.*
Proximate or Present Perfect,	بولا هے ,	*bolá hai.*
Remote or Past Perfect,	بولا تها ,	*bolá thá.*
Past Dubious,	بولا هو ,	*bolá ho.*
Past Presumptive,	بولا هوگا ,	*bolá hogá.*
Past Conditional or Optative, 3rd form,	بولا هوتا ,	*bolá hotá.*

VOCABULARY.

Urdu—English.

Adj., Adjective; adv., Adverb; n. m., Noun Masculine; n. f., Noun Feminine; v. int., Verb Intransitive; v. t., Verb Transitive; postp., Postposition; pron., Pronoun.

اب ,	*ab,*	adv.	now.
اب تک ,	*ab tak,*	”	up to now, yet, hitherto.
ابھی ,	*abhí,*	”	just now.
آپ ,	*áp,*	honorific pronoun, you, your honour.	

This same form is used in a reflexive sense, "self."

اِتنا ,	*itná,*	adj.	as much, so much.
اُتنا ,	*utná,*	adj.	so much.
اٹھ ,	*áṭh,*	adj.	eight.
اُٹھانا ,	*uṭháná,*	v. t.	to raise, lift up.
اُٹھنا ,	*uṭhná,*	v. int.	to rise, get up.
آج ,	*áj,*	adv.	to-day.
اجازت ,	*ijázat,*	n. f.	permission, leave.
اچّھا ,	*achchhá,*	adj.	good.
آخرکار ,	*ákhir kár,*	adv.	at last, finally.
آدمی	*ádmí,*	n. m.	man, human being.
اخبار ,	*akhbár,*	n. m.	news, newspaper.
اِدھر ,	*idhar,*	adv.	hither.
اُدھر ,	*udhar,*	adv.	thither.
ادھورا ,	*adhúrá,*	adj.	half done, incomplete.
آرام ,	*árám,*	n. m.	rest, ease.
آڑ ,	*áṛ,*	n. f.	shelter, covering.
اڑانا ,	*uṛáná,*	v. t.	to cause to fly.
اڑنا ,	*uṛná,*	v. int.,	to fly.
اڑھائی ,	*aṛháí,*	adj.	two and a half.

اِس ,	*is,*	formative of *yih.*	
اُس ,	*us,*	,, ,, *wuh.*	
اسباب ,	*asbáb,*	n. m.	effects, luggage, furniture.
استاد ,	*ustád,*	n. m.	teacher.
استاني ,	*ustání,*	n. f.	teacher (female).
استري ,	*istrí,*	n. f.	iron, (polishing).
اسمان ,	*ásmán,*	n. m.	sky, heaven.
افسوس ,	*afsos,*	n. m.	sorrow, alas !
اکيلا ,	*akelá,*	adj.	alone.
اگر ,	*agar,*	conj.	if.
اگرچه ,	*agarchi,*	conj.	although, even if.
اگر ,	*Agrá,*	s. m.	Agra.
اگے ,	*áge,*	adv.	before, in front of.
البتّه ,	*albatta,*	adv.	certainly, indeed.
الگ ,	*alag,*	adj. and adv., apart, separately.	
الماری ,	*almarí,*	n. f.	press, cupboard, book-case, wardrobe.
ام ,	*ám,*	n. m.	mango.
امسال ,	*imsál,*	adv.	this year.
انا ,	*áná,*	v. int., to come.	
اناج ,	*anáj,*	n. m.	grain.
اندر ,	*andar,*	postp., in, within, into.	
انڈا ,	*anḍá,*	n. m.	egg.
انتظار کرنا ,	*intizár karná,*	v. t.	to expect.
انگور ,	*angúr,*	n. m.	grape.
اواز ,	*áwáz,*	n. f.	voice, sound.
اوپر ,	*úpar,*	postp., over, above.	
اور ,	*and,* aur	conj.	and, also, other.
اوزار ,	*auzár,*	n. m.	(sing. and pl.), tools, weapons.

Khoti ká
áge

Kelá - banana

اولاد ,	*aulád,*	n. f.	children, offspring.
ایسا ,	*aisá, e,*	adj. and adv.,	so, thus, this way.
ایسانہ ہو کہ ,	*aisá na ho ki,*		so that it may not be that—lest.
ایک ,	*ek,*		one.
باپ ,	*báp,*	n. m.	father.
بات ,	*bát,*	n. f.	word, matter, thing.
بات چیت کرنا ,	*bát chít karná,*	v. t.,	to converse.
باربار ,	*bár bár,*	adv.	again and again, often.
بارود ,	*bárúd,*	n. f.	gunpowder.
بارہ ,	*bárah,*	adj.	twelve.
باغ ,	*bág,*	n. m.	garden.
بالکل ,	*bilkull,*	adv.	altogether, entirely.
بالنا ,	*bálna,*	v. t.	to light, (candle or lamp).
باندھنا ,	*bándhná,*	v. t.	to bind, fasten.
بانس ,	*báns,*	n. m.	bamboo.
باورچی ,	*báwarchí,*	n. m.	cook.
باہر ,	*báhar,*	adv.	outside.
بتانا ,	*batáná*	v. t	to show, point out.
بتادینا ,	*batá dená,*	v. t.	to show, point out.
بتّی ,	*battí,*	n. f.	wick, candle, lamp.
بچّا ,	*bachchá,*	n. m.	child, infant, baby.
بچھاونا ,	*bichhauna,*	n. m.	bed, bedclothes.
بہ دولت ,	*ba-daulat* (*kí*),	postp.,	by means of, favour of, prestige of.
بُرا ,	*bura,*	adj.	bad, evil, wicked.
برابر ,	*barábar,*	adv.	equally, regularly.
برخلاف ,	*barkhilaf* (*ke*),	adv. and postp.,	against, contrary, opposite to.

بڑا ,	*baṛá,*	adj. and adv., big, large, great, very.
بڑھئی ,	*baṛhaí,*	n. m. carpenter.
بزّاز ,	*bazzáz,*	n. m. draper, cloth-seller.
بعد ,	*b'ad,*	adv. and postp., after.
بعض ,	*b'az,*	adj. some, a few.
بغداد ,	*Bagdád,*	n. m. Bagdad.
بغیر ,	*bagair,*	postp. without.
بلانا ,	*buláná,*	v. t. to call.
بلالینا ,	*bulá lená,*	v. t. to call up.
بلکه ,	*balki,*	adv. and conj., but, but rather, moreover, on the contrary.
بنانا ,	*banáná,*	v. t. to make, cause to make.
بندکرنا ,	*band karná,*	v. t. to shut, close, stop.
بندوق ,	*banḍúq,*	n. f. gun.
بنّا ,	*banná,*	v. int., to be made, to become.
بنیا ,	*baniyá,*	n. m., shopkeeper, grain-seller.
بنیان ,	*banyán,*	n. m., singlet, vest.
بوتام ,	*botám,*	n. m., (English, corruption of) button.
بوجهه ,	*bojh,*	n. m., load, burden.
بولنا ,	*bolná,*	v. int., to utter sound, speak.
بونا ,	*boná,*	v. t. to sow.
بهات ,	*bhát,*	n. m., (boiled) rice.
بهاري ,	*bhárí,*	adj. heavy, weighty, important.
بهاگنا ,	*bhágná,*	v. int., to flee, escape.
بهاگ جانا ,	*bhág jáná,*	v. int., to flee away, escape.
بهائي ,	*bháí,*	n. m., brother.
بهت ,	*bahut,*	adj. and adv., much, many.

بهر ,	*bhar,*	adv.	fully, whole.
بهرا ,	*behrá,*	n. m.	(English) bearer.
بهروسا ,	*bharosá,*	n. m.	reliance, trust.
بهرنا ,	*bharná,*	v. t.	to fill, with *men,* of thing filled; or, with *se,* of thing with which filled.
بہن ,	*bahin,*	n. f.	sister.
بهوكها ,	*bhúkhá,*	adj.	hungry.
بهی ,	*bhí,*	conj.	also, too, and, even, with.
بهيتر ,	*bhítar,*	adv.	within, inside.
بهيجنا ,	*bhejná,*	v. t.	to send.
بهيكه مانگنا ,	*bhíkh mángná,*	v. t.	to beg.
بيان كرنا ,	*bayán karná,*	v. t.	to explain, relate, narrate.
بيٹا ,	*beṭá,*	n. m.	son.
بيٹی ,	*beṭí,*	n. f.	daughter.
بيٹهنا ,	*baiṭhná,*	v. int.	to sit.
بيٹهه جانا ,	*baith jáná,*	v. int.,	to sit down, be seated.
بيج ,	*bíj,*	n. m.	seed.
بےچاره ,	*be-chárá,*	adj.	poor, helpless, wretched.
بيچنا ,	*bechná,*	v. t.	to sell.
بيس ,	*bís,*	adj.	twenty, a score.
بے فائده ,	*be-fáida,*	adv.	in vain.
بيل ,	*bail,*	n. m.	ox, bullock.
بيمار ,	*bímár,*	n. m.	and adj., sick man, patient, sick.
بيوی ,	*bíwí,*	n. f.	lady, wife.
پار ,	*pár,*	postp.	and adv., across.
پاس ,	*pás,*	adj.	and adv., near, by, with.
پانا ,	*páná,*	v. t.	to find, get, obtain.

پانچ ,	*pán̲ch,*	adj.	five.
پاني ,	*pání,*	n. m.	water.
پهلا ,	*pahilá,*	adj.	first.
پهلے ,	*pahile,*	adv.	firstly.
پاےجامه ,	*páejáma,*	n. m.	drawers.
پتلون ,	*patlún,*	n. m.	trousers, " pantaloons."
پر ,	*par,*	postp.,	on, upon.
پر ,	*par,*	conj.	but, moreover, only.
پرچ ,	*pirich,*	n. m.	saucer.
پرسوں ,	*parson̲,*	adv.	day before yesterday, day after to-morrow.
پڑنا ,	*paṛná,*	v. int.	to lie, be lying.
پڑهانا ,	*paṛháná,*	v. t.	to teach, cause to read.
پڑهنا ,	*paṛhná,*	v. t.	to read aloud, recite, learn.
پس ,	*pas,*	conj. and adv.,	therefore.
پلانا ,	*piláná,*	v. t.	to cause to drink, give to drink.
پلٹن ,	*palṭan̲,*	n. f.	regiment.
پلس ,	*pulıs,*	n. m.	(Eng.) police.
پلنگ ,	*palang,*	n. m.	bedstead.
پنجرا ,	*pinjrá,*	n. m.	cage.
پنکها ,	*pan̲khá,*	n. m.	punkah, fan.
پونچهنا ,	*pochhná,*	v. t.	to wipe, to dust.
پوچهنا ,	*púchhná,*	v. t.	to ask, with *se.*
پونے ,	*paune,*	adj.	a quarter less than—
پهاوڑا ,	*pháwṛá,*	n. m.	mattock, spade.
پهٹنا ,	*phaṭná,*	v. int.,	to split, tear.
پهٹ جانا ,	*phaṭ jáná,*	v. int.,	to get split, be torn.
پهر ,	*phir,*	adv.	again.
پهل ,	*phal*	n. m.	fruit.

پہنچانا ,	*pahun̲chánú,*	v. t.	to send, bring, cause to arrive.
پہنچنا ,	*pahun̲chná,*	v. int.,	to arrive, reach.
پہننا ,	*pahinná,*	v. t.	to clothe with, dress.
پھول ,	*phúl,*	n. m.	flower.
پھینکنا ,	*phen̲kná,*	v. t.	to throw.
پھینکدینا ,	*phen̲k dená,*	v. t.	to throw away.
پیپا ,	*pípá,*	n. m.	canister, barrel, (Eng. pipe).
پیچھے ,	*píchhe,*	postp. and adv.,	behind, after.
پیالا ,	*piyálá,*	n. m.	cup.
پیسا ,	*paisá,*	n. m.	pice, money.
پیشاور ,	*Pesháwar,*	n. m.	Pesháwar.
پیلا ,	*pílá,*	adj.	yellow.
پینا ,	*píná,*	v. t.	to drink.
پی جانا ,	*píjáná,*	v. int.,	to drink up.
پی لینا ,	*pí lená,*	v. t.	to drink, "to take and drink."
تاکید ,	*tákíd kárná,*	v. t.	to insist, enjoin.
تاهم ,	*táham,*	conj.	nevertheless, still.
تاکه ,	*táki,*	conj.	in order that.
تب ,	*tab,*	adv.	then.
تجارت ,	*tijárat,*	n. f.	trade, commerce.
تجه ,	*tújh,*		formative of تو, *tú.*
تدبیر ,	*tadbír,*	n. f.	expedient, plan.
کرنا ,	,, *karná,*	v. t.	to arrange, contrive.
ترازو ,	*tarázu,*	s. m.	scales.
ترسوں ,	*tarson̲,*	adv.	three days ago, or hence.
ترکاری ,	*tarkárí,*	n. f.	vegetables, curry.
تشریف رکهنا ,	*tashríf rakhna,*	v. t.,	to be seated.

تشریف لے آنا ,	*tashríf le áná,*	v. int.,	to come.
لے جانا ,	„ *le jàná,*	v. int.,	to depart.
تسلی دینا ,	*tasallí dená,*	v. t.	to comfort, cheer.
تک ,	*tak,*	postp.,	up to.
تم ,	*tum,*	pron.	you.
تمہارا ,	*tumhárá,*	„	your.
تمہیں ,	*tumhen̲,*	„	you.
تنگ حال ,	*tang hál,*	n. m.	straits, necessitous circumstances.
تنہا ,	*tanhá,*	adv.	alone.
تو ,	*tú,*	pron.	thou.
تو ,	*to,*	conj.	then.
توبھی ,	*taubhí,*	conj.	nevertheless.
توڑنا ,	*toṛná,*	v. t.	to break, to gather (flowers or fruits).
توڑ ڈالنا ,	*ṭor ḍálná,*	v. t.	to break up, smash.
تولنا ,	*taulná,*	v. t.	to weigh.
تھا ,	*thá,*	v. int.,	was.
تھکنا ,	*thakná,*	v. int.,	to tire, be tired.
تھک جانا ,	*thak jáná,*	v. int.,	to get tired.
تیز ,	*tez,*	adj. and adv.,	swift, quickly.
تین ,	*tín,*	adj.	three.
نیار ,	*taiyár,*	adj.	ready, prepared.
تیوں ,	*tyún̲,*	adv.	just so.
ٹوٹنا ,	*tútná,*	v. int.,	to be broken.
ٹوپی ,	*ṭopí,*	n. f.	hat, cap.
ٹھیک ,	*ṭhík,*	adj. and adv.,	right, correct, correctly.
جاگنا ,	*jágná,*	v. int.,	to wake, be awake.
جانا ,	*jáná,*	v. int.,	to go, go away.
جاننا ,	*jánná,*	v. t.	to know.

جانور	*jánwar,*	n. m.	animal.
جب ,	*jab,*	adv.	when.
جتنا ,	*jitná,*	pron., adj. and adv., as much.	
جدا ,	*judá,*	adj. and adv., separate, alone.	
جدھر ,	*jidhar,*	adv.	whither.
جگہ ,	*jagah,*	n. f.	place.
جلد ,	*jald,*	adv.	quickly.
جمنا ,	*Jamná,*	n. f.	Jumna.
جنگل ,	*jangal,*	n. m.	wilderness, forest, weeds.
جو ,	*jo,*	pron.	who.
جو ,	,,	conj.	if.
جوتنا ,	*jotná,*	v. t.	to yoke, to plough.
جوتي ,	*jútí,*	n. f.	shoe.
جوڑا ,	*joṛá,*	n. m.	a pair, a suit of clothes.
جھاڑو ,	*jháṛú,*	n. m.	broom.
جھاڑو دینا ,	*jháṛú dená,*	v. t.	to sweep.
جہاں ,	*jahán̲,*	adv.	where.
جھٹ ,	*jhaṭ,*	adv.	immediately, at once.
جھوٹھ ,	*jhúṭh,*	n. m.	lie.
جیسے ,	*jaise,*	adv.	as.
جیوں ,	*jyún̲,*	adv.	just as.
چادر ,	*chádar,*	n. f.	sheet, tablecloth, wrapper.
چار ,	*chár,*	adj.	four.
چاول ,	*cháwal,*	n. m.	rice, (husked, ready for cooking).
چاهنا ,	*cháhná,*	v. t.	to desire, wish for.
چرنا ,	*charná,*	v. t.	to graze.
چڑهانا ,	*chaṛháná,*	v. t.	to lift up, to raise.
چڑهنا ,	*chaṛhná,*	v. int.,	to mount, ascend.

چڑیا ,	*chiṛiyá,*	n. f.	bird.
چگنا ,	*chugná,*	v. t.	to peck, to feed (as birds).
چلانا ,	*chaláná,*	v. t.	to cause to move, drive.
چلنا ,	*chalná,*	v. int.,	to move, to go along.
چلے جانا ,	*chale jáná,*	v. int.,	to go away.
چمچہ or چمچ ,	*chamach* or *chamcha,*	n. m.,	spoon.
چمکنا ,	*chamakná,*	v. int.,	to shine, glitter, glisten.
چنا ,	*chána,*	n. m.	"gram," chickpea.
چوٹ ,	*choṭ,*	n. f.	hurt, wound.
چولها ,	*chúlhá,*	n. m.	fireplace, stove.
چنانچہ ,	*chúnán̲chi,*	adv.	so that, so.
چونکہ ,	*chún̲ki,*	conj. and adv.,	inasmuch as, since.
چھٹّی ,	*chhuṭṭí,*	n. f.	freedom, relief, leave, holiday.
چھری ,	*chhuri,*	n. f.	knife.
چھرّا ,	*chharrá,*	n. m.	shot, small shot.
چھوٹا ,	*chhoṭá,*	adj.	small, little.
چھوڑنا ,	*chhoṛná,*	v. t.	to leave, release, forsake.
چهه ,	*chhah,*	adj.	six.
چیز ,	*chíz,*	n. f.	thing.
چیل ,	*chíl,*	n. f.	kite.
حاضر ,	*házir,*	adj.	present.
حاضری ,	*háziri,*	n. f.	presence, attendance, breakfast.
حال آن کہ ,	*hál-án-ki,*	adv.	whereas, now that, although.
حساب ,	*hisáb,*	n. m.	account, arithmetic.
حضور ,	*huzúr,*	n. m.	presence, "your honour."

حکم ,	*hukm,*	n. m.	order, command.
خبردار ,	*khabardár,*	adj.	careful, mindful.
خدمتگار ,	*khidmatgár,*	n. m.,	servant, especially table-servant.
خراب ,	*kharáb,*	adj.	bad, evil, wicked.
خریدنا ,	*kharídná,*	v. t.	to purchase, buy.
خطّ ,	*khaṭṭ,*	n. m.	letter, note.
خواه — خواه ,	*khwáh—khwáh,* conj., whether—or.		
خوب ,	*khúb,*	adj. and adv.,	well, beautiful, good.
خوفناک ,	*khaufnák,*	adj.	terrible, terrific, awful.
دام ,	*dám,*	n m.	price, cost.
داخل هونا ,	*dákhil hona,*	v. int.	(*men*), to enter.
داروغه ,	*dároga,*	n. m.	Inspector or Sub-Inspector of Police.
دانا ,	*dáná,*	n. m.	grain.
دب جانا ,	*dab jáná,*	v. int.,	to be crushed.
درخت ,	*darakhht,*	n. m.	tree, plant.
دارد ,	*dard,*	n. m.	pain.
درزن ,	*darzan,*	adj.	(Eng.) dozen.
درزي ,	*darzí,*	n. m.	tailor.
درست ,	*durust,*	adj. and adv.,	straight, level, correct.
درمیان ,	*darmiyán* (*ke*), adv. and postp., between, within.		
دروازه ,	*darwáza,*	n. m.	door.
دریا ,	*daryá,*	n. f. m.,	river, sea, flood.
دریافت کرنا ,	*duryáft karná* (*ko*), v. t., to ascertain.		
دري ,	*darí,*	n. f.	carpet.
دشمن	*dushman,*	n. m.	enemy.
دکهه ,	*dukh,*	n. m.	sorrow.

دکهنا ,	*dukhná,*	v. int.,	to ache.
دکهاي دينا ,	*dikhaí dená,*	v. int.,	to appear.
دفعه ,	*dafá,*	n. f.	turn, time.
دق کرنا ,	*diqq karná,*	v. t.	to make uncomfortable.
دل ,	*dil,*	n. m.	heart, soul.
دل بهلانا ,	*dil bahláná,*	v. t.	to amuse oneself.
دو ,	*do,*	adj.	two.
دوبنا ,	*dúbná,*	v. int.,	to sink, drown.
دوده ,	*dúdh,*	n. m.	milk.
دور ,	*dúr,*	adv.	far.
دوڑانا ,	*dauṛáná,*	v. t.	to cause to run or gallop.
دوڑنا ,	*dauṛná,*	v. int.,	to run.
دوست ,	*dost,*	n. m.	friend.
دوسرا ,	*dúsrá,*	adj.	second.
دوکان ,	*dúkán,*	n. f.	shop.
دولت منده ,	*daulatmand,*	adj.	rich, wealthy.
دوا ,	*dawá,*	n. f.	medicine.
دوات ,	*dawát,*	n. f.	inkpot.
دهان ,	*dhán,*	n. m.	rice, as seed or crop.
دهوبي ,	*dhobi,*	n. m.	washerman.
دهوپ ,	*dhúp,*	n. f.	sunshine, sun's heat.
دهونا ,	*dhoná,*	v. t.	to wash.
دکهانا ,	*dikháná,*	v. t.	to show.
ديکهنا ,	*dekhná,*	v. t.	to see, look at.
ديگچي ,	*degchi,*	n. f.	cooking-pot.
دير ,	*der,*	n. m.	delay, time.
ديوار ,	*díwár,*	n. f.	wall.
دهلي ,	*Dehli.*		
ڈاک ,	*ḍák,*	n. f.	post.
ڈهائي ,	*ḍháí,*	adj.	two and a half.

ڈیڑہ ,	*ḍerh,*	adj.	one and a half.
ذرد ,	*zard,*	adj.	yellow.
رات ,	*rát,*	n. f.	night.
راج مستري ,	*ráj mistrí,*	n. m.	mason, bricklayer.
راستہ ,	*rásta ,*	n. m.	way, road.

Rásta means road or *way to* a place, *ráh* means the same, but has also an ethical aspect. *Saṛak* is the material roadway on which one travels.

راہ دیکھنا ,	*ráh dekhná (ki),* v. t.,		to look for, expect.
رکھنا ,	*rakhná,*	v. t.	to keep, retain, hold.
رنگ ,	*rang,*	n. m.	colour, dye.
رنگانا	*rangáná,*	v. t.	to dye, colour.
رنگریز ,	*rangrez,*	n. m.	dyer.
روٹي ,	*roṭí,*	n. m.	bread.
روز ,	*roz,*	n. m.	day.
روز روز ,	*roz roz,*	adv.	day by day, every day.
روشني ,	*roshni or raushni,* n. f.,		light.
رومال ,	*rúmál,*	n. m.	handkerchief.
رونا ,	*roná,*	v. int.	to cry, weep.
رهنا ,	*rahná,*	v. int.	to remain, stay.
زبان ,	*zubán,*	n. f.	tongue, language.
زمين ,	*zamín,*	n. f.	earth, land.
زور ,	*zor,*	n. f.	power, violence (with *se*), strongly.
زين ,	*zín,*	n. m.	saddle.
سا ,	*sá,*	adj.	and adv. of similitude-like, —ish, very (?)
سابن ,	*sábun,*	n. m.	soap.
سات ,	*sát,*	adj.	seven.
ساتهہ ,	*sáth (ke),*	postp.,	with, in company of.
ساڑھے ,	*sáṛhe,*	adj.	—plus a half.

سال ,	*sál,*	n. m.	year.
سالن ,	*sálan,*	n. m.	meat-curry.
سامنے ,	*sámne* (*ke*),	postp.,	in front of, opposite.
سانپ ,	*sán̲p,*	n. m.	snake.
سائس ,	*sáis,*	n. m.	groom.
سب ,	*sab,*	adj.	all, every.
سپاهي ,	*sipáhí,*	n. m.	soldier, constable.
سچ ,	*sach,*	adj.	true.
سرخ ,	*surk̲h̲,*	adj.	red.
سر ,	*sir* or *sar,*	n. m.	head.
صرف و نحو ,	*sarf-o-nahw,*	n. f.	grammar (lit. accidence and syntax).
سرکار ,	*sarkár,*	n. m.	chief, "government."
سڑک ,	*saṛak,*	n. f.	road (the material road on which one travels), synn. *rásta* or *ráh*.
سزا ,	*sazá,*	n. f.	punishment.
سفيد ,	*sufaid* or *sufed,*	adj.,	white.
سلوک ,	*sulúk,*	n. m.	treatment (especially good).
سلوک کرنا ,	*sulúk karná* (with *se*),	v. t.,	to treat (esp. well), to behave to.
سمجها دينا ,	*samjhá dená,*	v. t.	to explain thoroughly, to cause to be understood.
سمجهنا ,	*samajhná,*	v. t.	to understand.
سنائي دينا ,	*sunáí dená,*	v. int.,	to be heard.
سنانا ,	*sunáná,*	v. t.	to cause to hear or be heard.
سننا ,	*sunná,*	v. t.	to hear.
سوداگر ,	*saudágar,*	n. m.	merchant, shopkeeper.

سونا ,	*soná,*	v. int.	to sleep.
سو جانا ,	*so-jana,*	v. int.	to sleep.
سوا ,	*sawá,*	adj.	a quarter more than—.
سوا ,	*siwá* (with *ke*),	postp.,	except.
سویرے ,	*sawere,*	adj. adv.,	early, in the early morning.
سہارا ,	*sahára,*	n. m.	support, reliance, help.
سے ,	*se,*	postp.	by, with, from, than.
سیب or سیو ,	*seb or se,o,*	n. m.	apple.
سیر ,	*ser,*	n. m.	a weight (abt. 2lbs.)
سیکھنا ,	*síkhná,*	v. t.	to learn.
سینا ,	*síná,*	v. t.	to sew.
سیاهي ,	*siyáhí,*	n. f.	ink, blacking.
شاباش ,	*shábásh,*	interj.,	bravo ! well done !
شاگرد ,	*shágird,*	n. m.	pupil, disciple.
شام ,	*shám,*	n. m.	evening.
شخص ,	*shakhs,*	n. m.	person, individual.
شروع کرنا ,	*shur'u karná* (*ko*),	v. t.,	to begin.
شکار کھیلنا ,	*shikár khelná,*	v. t.	to hunt, go shooting.
شہر ,	*shahr,*	n. m.	city, town.
شورو غل ,	*shor-o-gul,*	n. m.	noise and row.
صاحب ,	*sáhib,*	n. m.	(lit. lord of—) gentleman, master.
صرف ,	*sirf,*	adj. and adv.,	only, merely.
صندوق ,	*sandúq,*	n. m.	? f., box.
ضرور ,	*zarúr,*	adv.	necessarily, certainly.
ضرورت ,	*zarúrat,*	n. f.	necessity, need.
طرح ,	*tarah,*	n. f.	manner (with verbs "he does it *like* this").
طرف,	*taraf,*	s. f.	(and postp. with *kí*), side, direction.

تہ کرنا ,	*tah karná,*	v. t.	to fold, roll up, to dispose of (a case).
عرض کرنا ,	*'arz karná,* (with *kí* or *ko*), v. t., to report, state, request.		
عزّت ,	*'izzat,*	n. f.	honour, esteem, reputation.
عورت ,	*'aurat,*	n. f.	woman.
غافل ,	*gáfil,*	adj.	careless.
غریب ,	*garíb,*	adj. and n. m., poor, meek, poor man.	
غور کرنا ,	*gaur karná* (*par*), v. t., to reflect, meditate.		
فارسی ,	*Fársí,*	adj. and n. f., Persian people (m.), Persian language (f.).	
فدوی ,	*fidwi,*	n. m.	devotee, slave.
فرائض ,	*faráiz,*	n. m.	pl. of *farz,* duties, obligations.
فرمانا ,	*farmáná,*	v. t.	to command (used honorifically of merely saying or doing anything).
فصل ,	*fasl,*	n. f.	division, harvest, crop.
فقط ,	*faqt,*	adv.	only, merely.
فوراً ,	*fauran,*	adv.	immediately, at once, quickly.
فی الحال ,	*fílhál,*	adv.	in the (present) case, just now.
قاعدہ ,	*qá'ida,*	n. m.	rule, primer, alphabet book.
قبل ,	*qabl* (*ke*),	postp.,	before, previously.
قلم ,	*qalam,*	n. m.	(? f.) pen.
قمیض ,	*qamiz,*	n. m.	shirt, chemise.
قیمت ,	*qímat,*	n. f.	price.

کا ,	*ká,*	postp.,	of.
کاٹنا ,	*káṭná,*	v. t.	to cut, bite.
کارتوس ,	*kártús,*	n. m.	cartridge.
کافي ,	*káfí,*	adj.	enough, sufficient.
کالا ,	*kálá,*	adj.	black, dark.
کالر ,	*kálar,*	n. m.	collar (Eng.).
کانجي ,	*kánjí,*	n. f.	gruel, starch.
کاهے کو ,	*káhe ko,*	adv.	why? for what purpose?
کب ,	*kab,*	adv.	when?
کبهي ,	*kabhí,*	adj. and adv.,	ever.
	kabhí kabhí,	,,	sometimes.
	kabhí nahín	,,	never.
کپڑا ,	*kapṛá,*	n. m.	cloth, clothing.
کتاب ,	*kitáb,*	n. f.	book.
کتا ,	*kuttá.*	n. m.	dog.
کتنا ,	*kitná,*	adj. and adv.,	how much, how many.
کچهه ,	*kuchh.*	pron. and adv.,	some, any.
	,, *nahín,*		nothing.
کدهر ,	*kidhar,*	adv.	where? whither?
کرتا ,	*kurtá,*	n. m.	jacket, vest.
کرسي ,	*kursí,*	n. f.	chair, throne.
کرنا ,	*karná,*	v. t.	to do.
کرني ,	*karní,*	n. f.	trowel.
کروا ,	*karwá,*	adj.	bitter.
کروانا ,	*karwáná,*	v. t.	to cause to do.
کسنا ,	*kasna,*	v. t.	to bind, tighten.
کل ,	*kal,*	adv.	to-morrow, or yesterday.
کلام ,	*kalám,*	n. m.	word, saying.

کلف,	*kalaf* (or *kalap*),	n. m.,	starch.
کلکتہ,	*Kalkattá*,	n. m.	Calcutta.
کمربند,	*kamarband*,	n. m.	belt, girdle, waistband.
کمرہ,	*kamra*,	n. m.	chamber, room, apartment.
کنارا,	*kinárá*,	n. m.	edge, border, bank shore.
کون,	*kaun*,	pron.	who?
کوّا,	*kauwá*,	n. m.	crow.
کوچ کرنا,	*kúch karná*,	v. int.,	to set forth.
کہ,	*ki*,	conj.	that, so that.
کہاں,	*kahán*,	adv.	where?
کہانا,	*khánа́*,	v. t.	to eat.
کہا جانا,	*khá jáná*,	v. int.,	to eat up.
کہانا,	*khánа́*,	n. m.	food, dinner, meal.
کہچڑی,	*khichṛí*,	n. f.	a dish of rice and pulse.
کہرپی	*khurpí*,	n. f.	a kind of spud or garden trowel used by gardeners and grass-cutters.
کہڑا ہونا,	*khará honá*,	v. int.,	to be standing, to stand up.
کہِلنا,	*khilna*,	v. int.,	to open, bloom, as a bud.
کہُلنا,	*khulná*,	v. t.	to open.
کہنا,	*kahná*,	v. t.	to say, tell.
کہودنا,	*khodná*,	v. t.	to dig.
کہولنا,	*kholná*,	v. t.	to open, set open.
کہیت,	*khet*,	n. m.	field.
کیسا,	*kaisá*,	adj. and adv.,	how? what kind of?

کیا ,	*kyá,*	adj.	what ?
کیوں ,	*kyún,*	adv.	why ?
گاڑي ,	*gáṛí,*	n. f.	cart, carriage.
گالي دينا ,	*gálí dená,*	v. t.	(lit.) to "cheek," to abuse in obscene language.
گانا ,	*gáná,*	v. t.	to sing.
گدھا ,	*gadhá,*	n. m.	ass, donkey.
گذر جانا ,	*gu,zar jáná,*	v. int.,	to pass away, die.
گرانا ,	*giráná,*	v. t.	to throw down.
گرادينا ,	*girá dená,*	v. t.	do.
گرم ,	*garm,*	adj.	hot, warm.
گرنا ,	*girná,*	v. t.	to fall.
گرپڑنا ,	*gir paṛná,*	v. int.,	to fall down.
گلابي ,	*gulábí,*	adj.	rose-colour.
گلابند ,	*galaband,*	n. m.	necktie.
گلي ,	*galí,*	n. f.	a lane.
گننا ,	*ginná,*	v. t.	to count.
گو ,	*go,*	conj.	if.
گوکه ,	*go ki,*	,,	if indeed, although.
گورا ,	*gorá,*	adj. and n. m.,	fair, a fair man, esp. European soldier.
گوشت ,	*gosht,*	n. m.	flesh, meat.
گول مرچ ,	*gol mirch,*	n. f.	round or black pepper.
گھاس ,	*ghás,*	n. f.	grass, herbage.
گھر ,	*ghar,*	n. m.	house.
گھڑا ,	*ghaṛá,*	n. m.	jar, pot.
گھڑي ,	*ghaṛí,*	n. f.	watch, clock.
گھوڑا ,	*ghoṛá,*	n. m.	horse.
گھوڑي ,	*ghoṛí,*	n. f.	mare.
گھي ,	*ghí,*	n. m.	ghi, clarified butter.

گيند,	*gend,*	n. f.	ball.
گيند كهيلنا,	*gend khelná,*	v. t.	to play ball.
لادنا,	*ládná,*	v. t.	to load, lade.
لاكه,	*lákh,*	adj.	hundred thousand, a lakh.
لال,	*lál,*	adj.	red.
لال مرچ,	*lál mirch,*	n. f.	red pepper.
لانا,	*láná,*	v. int.,	to bring (contraction of *le-áná*).
لائق,	*láiq (ke),*	adv. and postp.,	worthy of, befitting, fit.
لدنا,	*ladná,*	v. int.,	to be loaded.
لڑائي,	*laṛáí,*	n. f.	fight, quarrel, battle.
لڑائي كرنا,	*laṛáí karná* (*se*),	v. t.,	to fight with or against.
لڑكا,	*laṛká,*	n. m.	boy.
لڑكي,	*laṛkí,*	n. f.	girl.
لغت,	*lugat,*	n. f.	dictionary.
لكڑي,	*lakṛí,*	n. f.	wood, stick.
لكهنا,	*likhná,*	v. t.	to write.
لگانا,	*lagáná,*	v. t.	to apply to, to place, spread, plant.
لگنا,	*lagná,*	v. int.,	to touch (physically or mentally), begin.
لوگ,	*log,*	n. m.	people, folk.
لے جانا,	*le jáná,*	v. int.,	to take away.
ليذا	*lená,*	v. t.	to take.
ليكن,	*lekin,*	conj.	but.
مارنا,	*márná,*	v. t.	to strike, kill.
مارڈالنا,	*már dálná,*	v. t.	to kill outright, violently murder.
مال,	*mál,*	n. m.	goods, possessions, wealth.

مالک,	*málik,*	n. m.	master.
ماهر هونا,	*máhir honá,*	v. int.	(with *men̲*), skilled in, proficient in.

N.B.—Platts says, with *se,* but all Indian scholars I have consulted say *men̲.*

مالی,	*málí,*	n. m.	gardener.
ماں,	*mán̲,*	n. f.	mother.
ماننا,	*mánná,*	v. t.	to mind, obey.
مانگنا,	*mángná,*	v. t.	to ask for.
مانند,	*mánind* (*kí*),	adv. and postp.,	like, resembling.
مبادا,	*mabádá,*	adv.	lest, that not.
مت.	*mat,*	adv.	don't.
مٹھائي,	*miṭhái,*	n. f.	sweets.
مچھلي,	*machhlí,*	n. m.	fish.
محنت,	*mihnat,*	n. f.	labour, work.
مدد,	*madad,*	n. f.	help, aid, assistance.
مدرسه,	*Madrasa,*	n. m.	school.
مرچا,	*mirchá,*	n. m.	red pepper.
مرد,	*mard ,*	n. m.	man (*vir,* as male or manly).
مرده,	*murda,*	adj. and n. m.,	dead, corpse.
مرغي,	*murgi,*	n. f.	hen, fowl.
مرنا,	*marná,*	v. int.,	to die.
مرجانا,	*mar jáná,*	v. int.,	do., "to go and die."
مزه دار,	*mazadár,*	adj.	tasty.
مزدور,	*mazdúr,*	n. m.	hired labourer, "coolie."
مزدوري,	*mazdúrí,*	n. f.	wages, hire.
مسافر,	*musáfir,*	n. m.	traveller, stranger.
مستري,	*mistrí,*	n. m.	(master-) workman.

مسجد,	*masjid,*	n. f.	place of prayer, mosque.
مشغول,	*mashgúl,*	adj.	engaged in, busy with.
مشکل,	*mushkil,*	adj.	difficult, hard.
معرفت,	*m'arifat (kí),*	postp.,	by means of, by the agency of.
مفت,	*muft,*	adv.	gratis, free, for nothing.
معلوم هونا,	*m'alúm honá,*	v. int.,	to be known.
مقدّمه,	*muqaddama,*	n. m.	case.
مگر,	*magar,*	conj.	only, but, except.
ملاحظه کرنا,	*muláhiza karná,*	v. t.,	to inspect.
ملانا,	*miláná,*	v. t.	to mix, cause to meet.
ملنا,	*milná,*	v. int.,	to meet with (with dat. of person), to be obtained.
مل جانا,	*mil jáná,*	v. int.,	to mix, meet.
ملنا,	*malná,*	v. t.	to rub.
ممکن,	*mumkin,*	adj.	possible.
من,	*man,*	n. m.	a maund=40 sers.
مناسب,	*munásib,*	adj.	fitting, proper, meet.
منشی,	*munshí,*	n. m.	writer, teacher (of Urdu and Persian).
منع کرنا,	*man'a karná,*	v. t.	to forbid, prohibit.
منگانا,	*mangáná,*	v. t.	to ask for, call for, order.
منّت کرنا,	*minnat karná (kí),*	v. t.,	to entreat, beseech.
منه,	*munh,*	n. m.	mouth, face.
موزه,	*moza,*	n. m.	sock, stocking.
معاف کرنا,	*mu'áf karná,*	v. t.	to forgive.
مولوي,	*maulví,*	n. m.	a Mohammadan doctor of law, a person learned in Arabic.

موافق,	*muwáfiq* (*ke*),	adv.	resembling, according to.
مہتر,	*mehtar,*	n. m.	sweeper.
میدان,	*maidan,*	n. m.	plain.
میز,	*mez,*	n. f.	table.
میں,	*main̲,*	pron.	I.
نہ,	*na,*	adv.	no, not.
نہ - نہ,	*na-na,*	adv.	neither—nor.
نتیجہ,	*natíja,*	n. m.	result.
نرسوں,	*narson̲,*	adv.	four days ago, or since.
نزدیک,	*nazdík* (*ke*),	postp.,	near.
نقصان,	*nuqsán,*	n. m.	loss.
نکلنا,	*nikalná,*	v. int.,	to go out, issue.
نماز,	*namáz,*	n. f.	prayer.
نماز پڑھنا,	*namáz paṛhná,*	v. t.,	to recite or say prayers.
نمک,	*namak,*	n. m.	salt.
نوکر,	*naukar,*	n. m.	servant.
نہایت,	*niháyat,*	adv.	exceedingly.
نہیں,	*nahín̲,*	adv.	no, not.
نیچے,	*níche* (*ke*),	postp.,	beneath, under.
نیز,	*níz,*	adv.	along with.
واجب,	*wájib,*	adj.	proper, fitting.
واسکت,	*wáskit,*	n. m.	(Eng.) waistcoat.
ورنہ,	*warna,*	adv.	if not, otherwise.
ووں,	*wūn̲,*	adv.	so.
وہ,	*wuh,*	pron.	he, she, it, that, they.
وہاں,	*wahán̲,*	adv.	there.
ویسا,	*waisá,*	adv.	so, in that manner.
ہاتھ,	*hāth,*	n. m.	hand.
حاضر ہونا,	*házir honá,*	v. int.,	to be present.

هال ,	*hál,*	n. m.	state, condition, account.
هال كمره ,	*hál kamra,*	n. m.	drawing-room.
هاں ,	*hán̲,*	adv.	yes.
هر ,	*har,*	adj. and adv.,	every.
هرگز نهيں ,	*hargiz nahín̲,*	adv.	never.
هرن ,	*harin,*	n. m.	deer, antelope.
هزار ,	*hazár,*	adj.	thousand.
هل	*hal,*	n. m.	plough.
هل جوتنا ,	*hal jotná,*	v. t.	to plough.
هم ,	*ham,*	pron.	we.
هميشه ,	*hamesha,*	adv.	always.
هنسنا ,	*han̲sná,*	v. int.,	to laugh.
هنوز ,	*hanoz,*	adv.	yet, still, up to now.
هوشيار ,	*hoshyár,*	adj.	vigilant, sensible.
هونا ,	*honá,*	v. int.,	to become, to be.
هوجانا ,	*ho jáná,*	v. int.,	to become.
هوں ,	*hún̲,*	v. int.,	I am.
هي ,	*hai,*	v. int.,	art, is.
يا ,	*ya,*	conj.	or.
ياتو - يا ,	*yá to-yá,*	conj.	either—or.
يعني ,	*ya'ní,*	adv.	that is to say.
يوں ,	*yún̲,*	adv.	thus.
يهه ,	*yih,*	pron.	he, she, it, these.
يهاں ,	*yahán̲,*	adv.	here.

ENGLISH—URDU.

The gender of nouns, and the "voices" of verbs are marked, as n. m., n. f., v. t., v. int.

abuse,	n. f.	*gálí,*	گالي
abuse, to	v. t.	*gálí dená,*	گالي دينا

accidence, n. m. *sarf,* صرف
N.B.—Sarf alone is masc., *sarf-o-nahw* together are fem.
according to, *ke muwáfiq,* کے موافق
account, n. m. *hisáb,* حساب
ache, to, v. int. *dukhná,* دکھنا
addition to (in) *ke a'láwa* or *'iláwa,* کے علاوہ
after, *ke ba'd,* کے بعد
,, *ke píchhe* کے پیچھے
again, *phir,* پھر
again and again, *bár bár,* بار بار
Agra, n. m. *Āgra,* اگرہ
aid, to, v. t. *madad karná,* مدد کرنا
alas! *afsos!* افسوس
all, *kull,* کلّ
,, *sab,* سب
,, *sárá,* سارا
alms, to ask, v. t., *bhíkh māngnā,* بھیکھ مانگنا
alone, (h) *akelá,* اکیلا
,, (p) *tanhā,* تنہا
alphabet-book, n. m. *qá'ida,* قاعدہ
although, *agarchi,* اگرچہ
,, *hál-án-ki,* حال ان کہ
,, *go ki,* گوکہ
altogether, *bilkull,* بال کلّ
always, *hamesha,* ہمیشہ
among, *ke darmiyán,* کے درمیان
,, *ke bích,* کے بیچ
amuse oneself, v. t., *ḍil bahlánā,* دل بہلانا
and, *aur, o,* اور او
and if not, *warna* ورنہ

animal, *jánwar*, جانور
antelope, *harin*, هرن
appear, v. int., *dikhaí dená*, دکهای دینا
,, ,, *nazar áná*, نظر انا
apple, *seb, seo*, سیو سیب
are, *hain*, هیں
arithmetic, *hisáb*, حساب
arrive, v. int., *pahunchná*, پہنچنا
,, cause to, v. t., *pahuncháná*, پہنچانا
,, ,, ,, *pahunchá dená*, پہنچادینا
as, *jaisá*, جیسا
as much as, *jitná*, جتنا
ascertain, v. t., *daryáft karná*, دریافت کرنا
ask (a question), v. int., *púchhná*, پوچھنا
ask (request), v. t., *mángná*, مانگنا
ass, *gadhá*, گدھا
assistance, n. f., *madad*, مدد
assist, v. t., *madad karná*, مدد کرنا
at last, *ákhir ko*, اخر کو
at once, *fauran*, فوراً
awake, (pres. part. of *jágná*), *jágtá*, جاگتا
awful, *khaufnák*, خوفناک
bad, *burá*, *kharáb*, خراب برا
Bagdad, n. m. *Bagdád*, بغداد
ball, n. f. *gend* گیند
bamboo, n. m. *báns*, بانس
bank (of a river), n. m., *kinára*, کنارہ
barrel, n. m., *pípá*, پیپا
be, become, v. int., *honá*, *ho jáná*, هوجانا
bearer, n. m., *behra*, بہرہ
because, *chūnki*, *kyūnki*, کیونکہ چونکہ

bedstead, n. m., *palang*, پلنگ
before (of place), *ke áge*, کے اگے
,, (of time), *ke* or *se*, *pahile*, کے یا سے پہلے
begin, v. t., *shuru' karná*, شروع کرنا
,, (in comp. with inf. formative). v. int., *lagná*,
bell, n. m., *ghanṭá*, گھنٹا
beneath, *ke níche* کے نیچے
beseech, v. t. (*kí*), *minnat karná*, منت کرنا
besides, *a'láwa*, علاوہ
between, *ke bích*, کے بیچ
,, *ke darmiyán*, کے درمیان
big, *baṛá*, بڑا
bind, v. t., *bándhná*, باندھنا
bird, n. f., *chiṛiyá*, چڑیا
bite, v. t., *káṭná*, کاٹنا
bitter, *kaṛwá*, کڑوا
black, *kálá*, *siyáh*, کالا سیاہ
blacking, blackness, n. f. *siyáhi*, سیاهي
bloom (as a flower), v. int., *khulná*, کھلنا
blow, n. f. *choṭ*, چوٹ
book, n. f. *kitáb*, کتاب
box, n. m. *sandúq*, صندوق
boy, n. m. *laṛká*, لڑکا
brave, *bahádur*, بہادر
bravo! *shábásh*, شاباش
bread, n. f. *roṭí*, روٹي
break, v. t. *toṛná*, (h) توڑنا
,, v. t. *shikast karná*, (p) شکست کرنا
breakfast, n. f. *házirí*, حاضري
bring, v. t. *láná*, *le áná*, لانا لے انا
,, (cause to come), v. t., *pahunchánná*, پہنچانا

bring (cause to come), v. t., *pahunchá dená,* پهنچادينا

broken (be), v. int., *túṭná, túṭ jáná,* توٹ جانا توٹنا

broom,   n. m.   *jhá,ú,* جهارا

brother,   n. m.   *bhái,* بهائى

build,   v. t.   *banáná,* بنانا

burden,   n. m.   *bojh,* بوجه

busy, to be, v. int., *mashgúl honā,* مشغول هونا

but, *lekin, magar, par,* پر - مگر - ليکن

butter, n. m.   *makkhan,* مکهن

button, n. m.   *botám,* بوتام

buy,   v. t.   *kharídná,* خريدنا

by, (near), *nazdik, pas, qarib* قريب - پاس - نزديک

by, (means of), *ke wasíb, ke maʻrifat,* كي معرفت کے وسيلے

cage,   n. m.   *pinjrá,* پنجرا

Calcutta, n. m.   *Kalkatta,* كلكتّا

call,   v. t.   *buláná,* بلانا

called, to be (named), v. t., *kabláná,* کهلانا

   ,,   (to oneself) or call and bring, v. t., *bulá lená,* بلالينا

cap,   n. f.   *ṭopí,* ٹوپي

careful, *hoshiyár* or *hoshyár,* هوشيار

careful, to be, v. t., *hoshiyárí karná,* هوشياري كرنا

careless, *gáfil,* غافل

carpenter, n. m.   *baṛhaí,* بڑهئي

carpet   n. f.   *darí,* دري

carriage, n. f.   *gáṛí,* گاري

cart,   ,,   ,,   ,,

cartridge, n. m.   *kartūs,* كارتوس

case (at law), n. m., *muqaddama,* مقدّمه

catch,   v. t.   *pakaṛná,* پكڑنا

chair,   n. f.   *kursí,* كرسي

chamber, n. m. *kamra*, كمره
chattels, n. m. *mál asbáb*, مال اسباب
cheer, to, v. t. *tasallí dená*, تسلّي دينا
chest, n. m. *sandūq*. صندوق
chief, n. m. *sardár*, سرادر
child, infant, n. m. *bachcha*, بچّه
children, offspring, n. m., *aulád*, اولاد
city, n. m. *shahr*, شہر
clean, *sáf*, ساف
clear, ,, ,,
clearly, *safáí se*, سفائی سے
climb, v. int., *charhná*, چڑھنا
cloth, n. m. *kaprá*, کپڑا
collar, n. m. *galáband*, گلابند
colour, n. m. *rang*, رنگ
come, v. int., *áná*, انا
comfort, to, v. t. *tasallí dená*, تسلّی دینا
command, n. m. *hukm*, حکم
,, to, v. t. *hukm dená*, حکم دینا
commerce, n. f. *tijárat*, تجارت
company (with), *ke sáth* کے ساتھہ
complete, *púrá, kámil, samúchá*, پورا, کامل, سموچا
completely, *bilkull*, بالکلّ
conformably, *bamujib*, به موجب
constable, n. m. *sipáhí*, سپاهی
continually, *barábar*, برابر
contrary, to, *bar khiláf*, برخلاف
converse, to, v. t. (*se*) (p) *guftogú karná*, گفت وگو کرنا
,, ,, ,, (h) *bát chít karná*, بات چیت کرنا
cook, n. m. *báwarchí*, باورچی

cook, to, v. t. *pakáná*, پکانا
cooking-pot, n. f. *degchí*, دیگچی
correct, *durust*, درست
count, v. t. *ginná*, گننا
crop, n. f. *fasl*, فصل
crow, n. m. *kauwá*, کوّا
crushed, to be, v. int. *dab jáná*, دب جانا
cry, weep, v. int. *roná*, رونا
cup, n. m. *piyálá*, پیالا
cupboard, n. f. *almárí*, الماری
curry (meat), n. m. *sálan*, سالن
,, vegetable, n. f. *tarkárí*, ترکاری
cut, v. t. *káṭná*, کاٹنا
daily, *roz roz, roz ba roz*, روز روز روز بروز
damage, n. m. *nuqsán*, نقصان
dark-complexioned, *kálá*, کالا
daughter, n. f. *beṭí*, بیٹی
day by day, see daily.
decidedly, *zarúr, albatta, beshakk*, ضرور البتّہ بےشک
deer, n. m. *harin*, ہرن
Dehli, p. n. *Dehli*, دہلی
delay, n. f. *der*, دیر
depart, v. int., *chale jana*, چلے جانا
,, ,, *tashrif le jáná*, تشریف لے جانا
descendant, n. m. *aulád*, اولاد
devotee, n. m. *fidwí*, فدوی
dictionary, n. f. *lugat*, لغت
did, v. t. *kiyá*, کیا
die, v. int., *marná*, مرنا
,, ,, *mar jáná*, مرجانا

die, pass away, v. int., *guzar jáná*, گذر جانا
difficult, difficulty, *mushkil*, مشکل
dig, v. t. *khodná*, کھودنا
dinner, n. m. *kháná*, کھانا
direction (of), *kí taraf*, کی طرف
disciple, n. m. *shágird*, شاگرد
distant, *dúr*, دور
do, v. t. *karná*, کرنا
dog, n. m. *kuttá*, کتّا
done, v. t. *kiyá*, کیا
donkey, n. m. *gadhá*, گدھا
doubtless, *beshakk*, بے شک
dozen, *darjan*, درجن
draper, n. m. *bazzáz*, بزّاز
drawers, n. m. *páejáma*, پاے جامہ
drawing-room, n. m. *gol kamra*, گول کمرہ
drink, v. t. *píná*, پینا
„ up, v. t. *pí jáná*, *pí lená*, پی لینا پی جانا
drive, v. t. *háñkná*, هانکنا
drown, v. int., *dúbná*, *dub jáná*, ڈوبنا ڈوب جانا
dust, to, (a room), v. t. *jhár poch karná*, جھاڑ پوچھہ کرنا
duty, duties, n. m. *farz*, *faraiz*, فرائض فرض
dye, v. t. *rangáná*, رنگانا
dyer, n. m. *rangrez*, رنگ ریز
early, *sawere*, سویرے
earth, n. f. *zamín*, زمین
eat, v. t. *kháná*, کھانا
eat up, v. t. *khá jáná*, کھاجانا
edge, n. m. *kinára*, کنارہ
egg, n. m. *andá*, انڈا

else, *aisá na ho ki,* ایسا نہ ہوکہ
,, *warna, nahín̲ to,* نہیں تو ورنہ
enemy, n. m. *dushman,* دشمن
enough, *káfí,* کافی
enquire, v. t., (h) *púchhná,* پوچھنا
,, (p) *daryáft karná,* دریافت کرنا
enter, v. int., *dákh̲il honá,* داخل ھونا
entreat, v. t. (*kí*) *minnat karná,* منّت کرنا
equal, to, equally, *ke barábar,* کے برابر
escape, v. int., *bhag jáná* or *nikalná,* بھاگ جانا بھاگ نکلنا
evening, n. m., *shám,* شام
every, *har ek,* ھر ایک
evil, (p) *kharáb* (h) *burá,* برا خراب
exactly, (h) *ṭhík se* (p) *durust,* ٹھیک سے درست
exceedingly, *niháyat,* نہایت
excellent, *u'mda,* عمدہ
except, *ke siwá,* کے سوا
explain, v. t. *bayán karná,* بیان کرنا
expect, v. t. (*ká*) *intizár karná,* انتظار کرنا
expedient, n. f., *tadbír,* تدبیر
face, n. f., *mun̲h,* منہ
facing, *ke muqabala,* کے مقابلہ
fair, *kh̲ūbsūrat,* خوبصورت
fall, v. int. *girná,* گرنا
fall, (to the lot of), v. int., *paṛná,* پڑنا
fall down, v. int., *gir parná,* گر پڑنا
fan, n. m. *pankhá,* پنکھا
fast, (make), v. t. *band karná,* بند کرنا
father, n. m. *báp,* باپ
field, n. m. *khet,* کھیت
fight, v. t. *laṛná, laṛáí karná,* لڑائی کرنا لڑنا

fighting, n. f. *laṛáí,* لڑای
fill, v. t. *bharná,* بھرنا
filled, to be, v. int., *bhar jáná,* بھرجانا
find, v. t. *páná,* پانا
fine, *khúb,* خوب
fire, n. f. *ág,* آگ
fire, (a gun), v. t., *bandúk chaláná* or *chhoṛná,*
بندوق چالانا - چھوڑنا
fire-place, stove, n. f. m., *chúlhá,* چولھا
fish, n. f. *machhlí,* مچھلی
fit, *ṭhík, taiyár,* تیار ٹھیک
fitting, *munásib,* مناسب
five, *pánch,* پانچ
flee, v. int., *bhágná, bhág jáná,* بھاگ جانا بھاگنا
flesh, n. m. *gosht,* گوشت
flower, n. m. *phúl,* پھول
fly, see flee.
forbid, v. t. *mana' karná,* منع کرنا
forgive, v. t. *mua'f karná,* معاف کرنا
forsake, v. t. *chhoṛná, chhoṛ dená,* چھوڑ دینا چھوڑنا
four, *chár,* چار
fourfold, *chauguná,* چوگنا
fowl, n. f. *murgí,* مرغی
friend, n. m. *dost,* دوست
front, in-of *ke sámne,* کے سامنے
fruit, n. m. (h) *phal,* (p) *mewa,* میوہ - پھل
full, *púrá, bhar,* بھر پورا
furniture, n. m. *asbáb,* اسباب
gallop, v. int. *dauṛná,* دوڑنا
„ cause to, v. t., *dauṛáná,* دوڑانا
garden, n. m. *bág,* باغ

gardener, n. m. *mální,* مالی
gave, v. t. *diyá,* دیا
gentleman, n. m. *sáhib,* صاحب
gently, (h) *dhíre dhíre,* (p) *ahista,* دھیرے دھیرے - آھستہ
get, obtain, v. t. *páná,* پانا
„ „ v. int., (with *ko*) *milná,* ملنا
get up, v. int., *uṭhná,* اٹھنا
give, v. t. *dená,* دینا
given, v. t. *diyá,* دیا
go along, v. int., *chalná,* چلنا
go away, v. int., *jáná, chale jáná,* جانا - چلے جانا
„ cause to, v. t. *chaláná,* چلانا
„ out, v. int., *nikal jáná,* نکل جانا
„ „ v. int., *báhar jáná,* باھر جانا
good, (h) *achchha,* (p) *u'mda,* اچّھا عمدہ
goods, n. m. *mál,* مال
gone, v. int., *gayá,* گیا
government, n. m. *sarkar,* سرکار
grain, n. m. *dáná, anáj,* دانا - اناج
gram, n. m. *chaná,* چنا
grammar, n. f. *sarf o nahw,* صرف و نحو
grass, n. f. *ghás,* گھاس
graze, v. t. *charná,* چرنا
„ cause to, v. t. *charáná,* چرانا
gratuitously, *muft,* مفت
green, (h) *hará,* (p) *sabz,* ھرا - سبز
groom, n. m. *sáis,* سائس
gruel, n. f. *kánjí,* کانجی
gun, n. f. *bandúq,* بندوق
gunpowder, n. f., *bárúd,* بارود

half, *ádhá*, ادھا
half done, *adhúrá*, آدھورا
hand, n. m. *háth*, هاتھ
handkerchief, n. m. *rúmál*, رومال
harm, n. m. *nuqsán*, نقصان
harvest, n. f. *fasl*, فصل
hat, n. f. *ṭopí*, ٹوپی
have to do, v. int., (*ko*) *karná paṛná*, کرنا پڑنا
he, *yih, wuh*, وہ
head, n. m. *sir*, سر
hear, v. t. *sunná*, سنا
heard (be) v. int., *sunáí dená*, سنائی دینا
heaven, n. m. *ásmán*, اسمان
heavy, *bhárí*, بھاری
help, v. t. (*kí*) *madad karná*, مدد کرنا
helpless, *bechára*, بے چارہ
hen, n. f. *murgí*, مرغی
hence, *is liya, is wāsṭe*, اس لئے - اس واسطے
here, *yahán*, یہاں
hither, *idhar*, ادھر
hitherto, (h) *abtak*, (p) *hanoz*, ابتک - هنوز
hold, v. t. *pakaṛná*, پکڑنا
holiday, n. f. *chhuṭṭí*, چھٹی
Honour, your, *huzúr*, حضور
honour, n. f. *i'zzat*, عزت
horse, n. m. *ghoṛá*, گھوڑا
hot, *garm*, گرم
hour, n. m. *ghanṭá*, گھنٹا
house, n. m. *ghar, makán*, گھر - مکان
how, *kaísá*, کیسا

how much, *kitná,* کتنا
hungry, *bhúkhá,* بهوکها
hunt, v. t. *shikár khelná,* شکار کهیلنا
hurt, v. t. *choṭ lagáná,* چوٹ لگانا
if, (p) *agar,* (h) *jo,* اگر جو
immediately, *fauran,* فوراً
important, *bhárí,* بهاری
inculcate, v. t. *samjhá dená,* سمجها دینا
indicate, v. t. *batáná,* بتانا
infant, n. m. *bachcha,* بچّه
ink, n. f. *siyáhí,* سیاهی
inkstand, inkpot, n. f., *dawát,* دوات
insist, v. t. *tákíd karná,* تاکید کرنا
inspect, v. t. *muláhiza karná,* ملاحظه کرنا
Inspector (of police), n. m., *dároga,* داروغه
invalid, n. m. *maríz, bímár,* مریض - بیمار
iron (laundry), n. f. *istrí,* استری
is, v. int. *hai,* هے
issue, offspring, n. m. *aulád,* اولاد
it, *yih, wuh,* یه - وه
jacket, n. m. *kurtá,* کرتا
Jumna, p. n. *Jamná,* جمنا
khicharí, n. f. *khicharí,* کهچڑی
kill, v. t. *márná, már ḍálná,* - مارنا مارڈالنا
kite, n. f. *chíl,* چیل
knife, n. f. *chhurí,* چهری
know, v. t. *jánná,* جاننا
known, to be, v. int., (*ko*) *ma'lūm honá,* معلوم هونا
labour, n. f. *mihnat,* محنت
labourer (hired) n. m. *mazdúr,* مزدور

lacking, (without),   *ke bagair,* بغیر کے

lacking, (incomplete),   *báqí,* باقی

lady,   n. f.   *bíwí* بیوی

lamp,   n. m.   *chirág,* چراغ

     (The English word lamp is also used.)

land, n. f.   *zamín,* زمین

lane, n. f.   *galí,* گلی

language,   n. f.   *zábán,* زبان

   ,,   bad, n. f.   *gálí,* گالی

large,   *baṛá,* بڑا

laugh,   v. int.,   *hansná,* ہنسنا

law, (doctor of), n. m.   *maulví,* مولوی

learn (to acquire knowledge), v. t., *síkhná,* سیکھنا

   ,,   (to study), v. t.   *paṛhná,* پڑھنا

learned man, n. m.   *'álim,* عالم

leave,   v. t.   *chhoṛná,* چھوڑنا

leave (of absence), n. f.   *chhuṭṭí,* چھٹّی

lentils, n. f.   *dál,* دال

lest,   *aisá na ho ki, mabáda,* مبادا - ایسا نہ ہوکہ

let go, v. t.   *chhoṛ dená,* چھوڑ دینا

let, (permit, allow), v. t.   *karne dená,* کرنے دینا

letter,   n. m.   (p) *khatt,* خطّ

   ,,   n. f.   (h) *chiṭṭhí,* چٹّھی

lie,   n. m.   *jhúṭh,* جھوٹھ

lies, to tell, v. int.   *jhúṭh bolná,* جھوٹھ بولنا

lift, v. t.   *uṭháná,* اٹھانا

light, (a lamp), v. t.   *bárná, jaláná,* جلانا - بارنا

light,   n. f.   *roshní,* روشنی

like,   *kí mánind,* کی مانند

live,   v. int., (p) *zinda honá,* (h) *jíná,* جینا - زندہ ہونا

load, n. m. *bojh*, بوجھ
load, to, v. t. *ládná*, لادنا
loaded, to be, v. int. *ladná*, لدنا
look, v. t. *dekhná*, دیکھنا
,, v. t. *dekh lená*, دیکھ لینا
look for, v. t. *talásh karná*, تلاش کرنا
loss, n. m. *nuqsán*, نقصان
lying, resting, (part of *paṛná*) *paṛá*, پڑا
make, v. t. *banáná*, بنانا
man, (*homo*), n. m. *ádmi*, آدمی
man, (*vir*), n. m. *mard*, مرد
mango, n. m. *ám*, آم
many, *bahut*, بہت
mare, n. f. *ghoṛí*, گھوڑی
margin, n. m. *kinára*, کنارہ
market, n. m. *bázár*, بازار
mason, n. m. *ráj mistrí*, راج مستری
matter, n. f. (h) *bát*, بات
,, n. m. (p.), *mu'ámala*, معاملہ
mattock, n. m. *pháwṛá*, پھاوڑا
maund, n. m. *man*, من
by means of, *kí m'arifat*, کی معرفت
,, *ke wasile se*, کے وسیلے سے
meat, n. m. *gosht*, گوشت
medicine, n. f. *dawá*, دوا
meditate, v. t. *gaur karná*, غور کرنا
meet, v. int., *milná*, ملنا
merchant, n. m. *saudágar*, سوداگر
midnight, n. f. *ádhí rát*, آدھی رات
in the midst, *ke darmiyán*, کے درمیان
milk, n. m. *dúdh*, دودھ

mind,	n. f.	*'aql,*	عقل
mind, to,	v. t.	*mánná,*	مانا
money,	n. m.	*rupáye,*	روپائے
month,	n. m.	*mahína,*	مہینہ
moreover,		*balki,*	بلکہ
mosque,	n. f.	*masjid,*	مسجد
mother,	n. f.	*mán̲,*	ماں
mount up,	v. int.,	*chaṛh jáná,*	چڑھ جانا
much,		*bahut,*	بہت
nay, rather,		*balki,*	بلکہ
near,		*nazdík,*	نزدیک
necessarily,		*zarúr,*	ضرور
necessity,	n. f.	*zarúrat,*	ضرورت
necktie,	n. m.	*galáband,*	گلا بند
need,	n. f.	*zarúrat,*	ضرورت
needle,	n. f.	*súí,*	سوئي
never,		(h) *kabhi nahín̲.*	کبھی نہیں
,,		(p) *hargiz nahín̲,*	هرگز نہیں
news,	n. f.	*khabár,*	خبر
newspaper,	n. m.	*akhbár,*	اخبار
no, not,		*nahín̲,*	نہیں
noise,	n. m.	*shor o gul,*	شور و غل
noon,		*do pahar,*	دوپہر
nothing,		*kuchh nahín̲,*	کچھ نہیں
now, just now,		*ab, abhí,*	اب - ابھی
till now,		*ab tak,*	اب تک
nowadays,		*āj kal,*	اج کل
obey,	v. t.	*manná,*	مانذا
obligation,	n. m.	*farz,*	فرض
obtain,	v. t.	*páná, hásil karná,*	حاصل کرنا پانا
one,		*ek,*	ایک

only,		*sirf, faqat,*	فقط - صرف
open, (as a flower),	v. int.,	*khilná,*	کھلنا
open,	v. int.,	*khulná,*	کھُلنا
open,	v. t.	*kholná,*	کھولنا
or,		*yá,*	یا
order,	n. m.	*hukm,*	حکم
order, to,	v. t.	*hukm dená,*	حکم دینا
otherwise,		*warna,*	ورنہ
out, outside,		*báhar,*	باہر
ox,	n. m.	*bail,*	بیل
pain,	n. m.	*dard,*	درد
pantaloon,	n. m.	*patlún,*	پتلون
pass away,	v. int.,	*guzar jáná,*	گذر جانا
patient,	n. m.	*maríz,*	مریض
pebbles,	n. m.	*kankaṛ,*	کنکڑ
peck,	v. t.	*chugná,*	چگنا
pen,	m. f. (?),	*qalam,*	قلم
people,	n. m.	*log,*	لوگ
pepper,	n. f.	*mirch,*	مرچ
permission,	n. f.	*ijázat,*	اجازت
Persian,	n. f.	*Fársí,*	فارسی
person,	n. m.	*shakhs,*	شخص
Peshawar,	n. m.	*Pesháwar,*	پیشاور
petition,	n. f.	*'arzí,*	عرضی
pice,	n. m.	*paisá,*	پیسا
pick up,	v. t.	*uṭháná,*	اٹھانا
pink,	adj.	*gulábí,*	گلابی
place,	n. f.	*jagah,*	جگہ
plain,	n. f.	*maidán,*	میدان
plan,	n. f.	*tadbir,*	تدبیر

plant, v. t. *lagáná,* لگانا
plough, n. m. *hal,* هل
,, to, v. t. *hal jotna,* هل جوتنا
point out, v. t. *batáná,* بتانا
police, n. m. "*pulis*" پلس
policeman, n. m. *sipáhí,* سپاهی
poor, indigent, (n. and adj.), *garíb,* غریب
poor, helpless, (n. and adj.), *bechára,* بے چارہ
possible, *mumkin,* ممکن
post (office), *ḍák, ḍák khána,* ڈاک خانہ ڈاک
pot, n. m. *ghaṛá,* گھڑا
prayer, to say, v. t., *namáz paṛhná,* نماز پڑھنا
prayers, liturgy, n. f., *namáz,* نماز
prepare, v. t. *taiyár karná,* تیار کرنا
prepared, ,, *taiyár,* تیار
present, *házir,* حاضر
press, cupboard, n. f., *almárí,* الماری
price, n. m. (h), *dám,* دام
,, n. f. (p), *qímat,* قیمت
primer, n. m. *q'aida,* قاعدہ
proficient, (*meṉ*) *máhir* ماهر
proper, *munásib,* مناسب
property, n. m. *mál, asbáb,* مال اسباب
pulse, n. f. *dál,* دال
punish, v. t. *sazá dená,* سزا دینا
pupil, n. m. *shagird,* شاگرد
put, place, v. t. *rakhná,* رکھنا
put on, v .t. *pahinná,* پہننا
quarrel, v. t. *laṛáí karná,* لڑائی کرنا
quickly, *jald,* جلد
raise, v. t. *uṭhánā,* اٹھانا

rather, *balkí,* بلکہ

read, to oneself, v. t., *dekhná,* دیکھنا

read, aloud, v. t. *paṛhná,* پڑھنا

ready, *taiyár,* تیار

reason, *sabab,* سبب

receive, v. t. *páná,* پانا

red, *lál,* لال

regularly, *barábar,* برابر

release, v. t. *chhoṛ dená,* چھوڑدینا

reliance, n. m. *bharosá,* بھروسا

represent, report (case), v. t., *'arz karná,* عرض کرنا

require, v. t. *cháhná,* چاہنا

rest, n. m. *árám,* ارام

result, n. m. *natíja,* نتیجہ

rice, grain, crop, n. m., *dhán,* دھان

,, ready for cooking, n. m., *cháwal,* چاول

,, cooked, n. m., *bhát,* بھات

rich, *daulatmand,* دولت مند

rider, n. m., *sawár,* سوار

ride, v. int., *sawar hona,* سوار ہونا

rise, v. int., *uṭhná,* اٹھنا

river, n. m. *daryá,* دریا

road, way to a place, n. m., *rásta,* راستہ

road, material road, n. f., *saṛak,* سڑک

room, n. m. *kamrá,* کمرہ

rose-coloured, *gulábí,* گلابی

rub, v. t. *malná,* ملنا

run, v. int., *dauṛná,* دوڑنا

,, cause to, v. t., *dauṛáná,* دوڑانا

,, away, v. int., *dauṛ jáná,* دوڑجانا

rupee,	n. m.	*rupiya,*	روپئه
saddle,	n. m.	*zín,*	زین
salt,	n. m.	*namak,*	نمک
salute,	v. t.	*salám karná,*	سلام کرنا
sash,	n. m.	*kamarband,*	کمربند
saucer,	n. m.	*pirich,*	پرچ
say,	v. t. (*se*),	*kahná,*	کهنا
scales,	n. m.	*tarázú,*	ترازو
school,	n. m.	*Madrasa,*	مدرسه
schoolmaster,	n. m.	*ustád,*	استاد
schoolmistress,	n. f.,	*ustání,*	استانی
sea,	n. m.	*daryá,*	دریا
second,		*dusrá,*	دوسرا
see,	v. t.	*dekhná,*	دیکهنا
seed,	n. m.	*bij,*	بیج
sell,	v. t.	*bechná,*	بیچنا
send,	v. t.	*bhejná,*	بهیجنا
separate,		*alag, judá,*	الگ جدا
separately,		*alag, judá,*	الگ جدا
ser,		*ser,*	سیر
servant,	n. m.	*naukar,*	نوکر
set forth,	v. t.	*bayán kárná,*	بیان کرنا
settle,	v. t.	*tah karná,*	ته کرنا
seven,		*sát,*	سات
sew,	v. t.	*síná,*	سینا
she,		*wuh,*	وه
sheet,	n. f.	*chádar,*	چادر
shelter,	n. f.	*ár,*	آڑ
shine,	v. int.,	*chamakná,*	چمکنا
shirt,	n. m.	*qamíz,*	قمیض

shoe, n. f. *júṭí*, جوتی

shoot, v. t. *bandúq chalána*, بندوق چلانا

shop, n. f. *dúkán*, دوکان

shopkeeper, n. m., *baniyá*, بنیا

show, v. t. *dikhána*, دکھانا

show, (itself), v. int., *dikhái dená*, دکھائی دینا

sick, n. m. *bímár*, *maríz*, مریض, بیمار

since, *chú<u>n</u>ki*, چونکہ

sing, v. t. *gáná*, گانا

sink, v. int. *dúbná*, ڈوبنا

sister, n. f. *bahin*, بہن

sit, v. int., *baiṭhná*, بیٹھنا

six, *chahh*, چھہ

sky, n. m. *ásmán*, اسمان

slay, slaughter, v. t., *máṛ ḍálná*, مارڈالنا

sleep, v. int., *soná*, *sojáná*, سوجانا - سونا

small, *chhotá*, چھوٹا

smash, v. t. *toṛ ḍálná*, توڑ ڈالنا

snake, n. m. *sámp*, سانپ

so, adj. and adv., *aisá waisá*, ویسا - ایسا

so, conj. *chunán<u>n</u>chi*, چنانچہ

sock, n. m. *moza*, موزہ

soldier, n. m. *sipáhi*, سپاہی

solicit, v. t. *'arz karná*, عرض کرنا

some, *kuchh*, کچھ

sometimes, *kabhí kabhí*, کبھی کبھی

sometime or other, *kabhí na kabhí*, کبھی نہ کبھی

son, n. m. *betá*, بیٹا

sorrow, n. m. (n) *dukh* (p) *afsos*, افسوس - دکھہ

sound, n. f. *áwáz*, اواز

sow,	v. t.	*boná,*	بونا
spade, mattock,	n. m.,	*phawṛá,*	پھاوڑا
speak,	v. int.,	*bolná,*	بولنا
spend,	v. t.	*kharch karná,*	خرچ کرنا
split,	v. int.,	*phaṭná,*	پھٹنا
spoilt,		*kharáb,*	خراب
spoon,	n. m.	*chamach,*	چمچ
stand,	v. int.,	*khaṛá honá,*	کھڑا ہونا
starch,		*kalaf* (m) *kánji* (f),	کلف - کانجی
state, to,	v. t.	*'arz karná,*	عرض کرنا
stay,	v. int.,	*ṭhahaṛná,*	ٹھہڑنا
still, yet,		(h) *taubhi,* (p) *táham,*	توبھی - تاھم
store,	n. f.	*dúkán,*	دوکان
straight,		(h) *sídha,* (p) *durust,*	سیدھا - درست
straighten,	v. t.	*do. with karná,*	کرنا — —
strike,	v. t.	*márná,*	مارنا
sufficient,		*káfí,*	کافی
suit, of clothes,	n. m.,	*joṛá,*	جوڑا
sunshine,	n. f.	*dhúp,*	دھوپ
support,	n. m.	*sahárá,*	سہارا
,,	v. t.	,, *dená,*	دینا—
syntax,	n. f.	*nahw,*	نحو
sweep,	v. t.	*jháṛú dená,*	جھاڑو دینا
sweetmeats,	n. f.	*miṭháí,*	مٹھائی
swiftly,		*jald,*	جلد
table,	n. f.	*mez,*	میز
tailor,	n. m.	*darzí,*	درزی
take,	v. t.	*lena,*	لینا
,, up,	v. t.	*uṭháná,*	اٹھانا
,, away,	v. int.,	*le-jáná,*	لے جانا

tasty, *maza dár* مزہ دار

teacher, m. n. m. *ustád,* استاد

,, f. n. f. *ustání,* استانی

teach, a matter, v. t., *sikháná,* سکھانا

teach, a subject, v. t., *paṛháná,* پڑھانا

tell, v. t. *kahná, batáná,* کہنا بتانا

terrible, *khaufnák,* خوفناک

then, *tab, to,* تو - تب

there, *wahán,* وہاں

therefore, *to, is liye,* اس لئے - تو

these, *yih,* یہ

thing, n. f. *chíz,* چیز

think, v. int., *sochná,* سوچنا

,, upon, v. t. (par), *gaur karná,* غور کرنا

thief, n. m. *chor,* چور

this, *yih,* یہ

those, *wuh,* وہ

three, *tín,* تین

throw away, v. t., *phenk dená,* پھینک دینا

,, down, v. t., *girá dená,* گرادینا

tighten, v. t. *kasná,* کسنا

time, n. m. *waqt,* وقت

tin (canister), n. m., *pípá,* پیپا

tired, to be, v. int., *thak jáná,* تھک جانا

to-day, *áj,* آج

toil, n. f. *mihnat,* محنت

,, to, v. t. ,, *karná,* —کرنا

to-morrow, *kal,* کل

tongue, n. f. *zubán,* زبان

torn, to be, v. int., *phaṭ jáná,* پھٹ جانا.

totally,		*bilkull,*	بالکّل
touch,	v. int.,	*ko lagná,*	کو لگنا
towards,		*kí taraf,*	کی طرف
trade,	n. f.	*tijárat,*	تجارت
traveller,	n. m.	*musáfir,*	مسافر
treat,	v. t.	*sulúk karná,*	سلوک کرنا
treatment,	n. m.	*sulúk,*	سلوک
trousers,	n. m.	*patlún,*	پتلون
trowel, mason's,	n. f.,	*karní,*	کرنی
,, gardener's,	n. f.,	*khurpí,*	کھرپی
true,	n. m.	*sach,*	سچ
truth, tell the,	v. int.,	*sach bolná,*	سچ بولنا
turn,	v. int.	*phirná,*	پھرنا
two,		*do.*	دو
under,		*ke níche,*	کے نیچے
understand,	v. t.	*samajhná,*	سمجھنا
unless,		*warna,*	ورنہ
uselessly,		*befaida,*	بے فائدہ
vainly,		,,	
very,		*bahut,*	بہت
vest,	n. m.	*kurtá,*	کرتا
vigilance,	n. f.	*hoshiyárí,*	ہوشیاری
vigorously,		*zor se,*	زور سے
voice,	n. f.	*áwáz,*	اواز
wall,	n. f.	*díwár,*	دیدار
warm,		*garm,*	گرم
was,	v. int.,	*thá,*	تھا
wash,	v. t.	*dhoná,*	دھونا
washerman,	n. m.,	*dhobí,*	دھوبی
waistcoat,	n. (?),	"*wáskit,*"	واسکٹ

water,	n. m.	*pání,*	پانی
way,	n. m.	*rástá,*	راستہ
wedding,	n. f.	*shádí,*	شادی
weed,	n. m.	*jangal,*	جنگل
weep,	v. int.,	*roná,*	رونا
weigh,	v. t.	*taulná,*	تولنا tolna
weighty,		*bhári,*	بھاری
well,		*achchhí tarah se,*	اچھی طرح سے
,,		*<u>kh</u>úb,*	جوب
well done!		*shábash,*	شاباش
were,	v. int.,	*the,*	تھے
what?		*kiyá,*	کیا
wheat,	n. m.	*gehún,*	گیہوں
whereas,		*chúnki,*	چونکہ
white,		*sufaid,*	سفید
who, which, what?		*kaun,*	کون
whole,		*sárá, bhar,*	بھر - سارا
why?		*kyún,*	کیوں
wick,	n. f.	*battí,*	بتّی
wife,	n. f.	*bíwí,*	بیوی
wipe,	v. t.	*pochhná,*	پوچھنا
wise,	n. m.	*'aql mand,*	عقل مند
with,		*ke sáth,*	کے ساتھ
within,		*bhítar,*	بھیتر
without,		*báhar,*	باھر
woman,	n. f.	*'aurat,*	عورت
woodland,	n. m.	*jangal,*	جنگل
work,	n. m.	*kám,*	کام
workman,	n. m.	*mazdúr,*	مزدور
worthy,		*láiq,*	لائق

wound,	n. f.	*choṭ,*	چوٹ
wrapper,	n. f.	*chádar,*	چادر
write,	v. t.	*likhná,*	لکھنا
writer,	n. m.	*munshí,*	منشی
year,	n. m.	(p), *sal,*	سال
,,	,,	(h), *baras,*	برس
this year,		*imsál,*	امسال
last year,		*pár sál,*	پارسال
next year,		*sál áyanda,*	سال آینده
yesterday,		*kal,*	کل
yoke, to,	v. t.	*jotná,*	جوتنا

Baptist Mission Press, Calcutta.